INVISIBLE HELPERS

CHARLES WEBSTER LEADBEATE

Paperback: 978-939492468-0

Any references to historical events, real people, or real places are used fictitiously. Names, characters, and places are products of the author's imagination.

Printed by:

Sanage Publishing House LLP

Mumbai, India

sanagepublishing@gmail.com

Charles Webster Leadbeater (16 February 1854 – 1 March 1934) was a member of the Theosophical Society, Co-Freemasonry, author on occult subjects and co-initiator with J. I. Wedgwood of the Liberal Catholic Church.

Originally a priest of the Church of England, his interest in spiritualism caused him to end his affiliation with Anglicanism in favour of the Theosophical Society, where he became an associate of Annie Besant. He became a high-ranking officer of the Society and remained one of its leading members until his death in 1934, writing over 60 books and pamphlets and maintaining regular speaking engagements.

CONTENTS

1. The Universal Belief In Them 5

2. Some Modern Instances 8

3. A Personal Experience 14

4. The Helpers 19

5. The Reality of Superphysical Life 25

6. A Timely Intervention 28

7. The "Angel Story." 31

8. The Story Of A Fire 36

9. Materialization And Repercussion 40

10. The Two Brothers 45

11. Wrecks And Catastrophes 51

12. Work Among The Dead 55

13. Other Branches Of The Work 64

14. The Qualifications Required 67

15. The Probationary Path 74

16. The Path Proper 80

17. What Lies Beyond 87

CHAPTER I

The Universal Belief In Them

It is one of the most beautiful characteristics of Theosophy that it gives back to people in a more rational form everything which was really useful and helpful to them in the religions which they have outgrown. Many who have broken through the chrysalis of blind faith and mounted on the wings of reason and intuition to the freer, nobler mental life of more exalted levels, nevertheless feel that in the process of this glorious gain a something has been lost - that in giving up the beliefs of their childhood they have also cast aside much of the beauty and the poetry of life.

If, however, their lives in the past have been sufficiently good to earn for them the opportunity of coming under the benign influence of Theosophy, they very soon discover that even in this particular there has been no loss at all, but an exceeding great gain - that the glory and the beauty and the poetry are there in fuller measure than they had ever hoped before, and no longer as a mere pleasant dream from which the cold light of common-sense may at any time rudely awaken them, but as truths of nature which will bear investigation - which become only brighter, fuller and more perfect as they are more accurately understood.

A marked instance of this beneficent action of Theosophy is the way in which the invisible world (which, before the great wave of materialism engulfed us, used to be regarded as the source of all living help) has been restored by it to modern life. All the charming folklore of the elf, the brownie, and the gnome, of the spirits of air and water, of the forest, the mountain, and the mine, is shown by it to be no more meaningless superstition, but to have a basis of actual and scientific fact behind it. Its answer to the great fundamental question "If a man die, shall he live again?" is equally definite and scientific, and its teaching on the nature and conditions of the life after death throws a flood of light upon much that, for the Western world at least, was previously wrapped in impenetrable darkness

It cannot be too often repeated that in this teaching as to the immortality of the soul and the life after death, Theosophy stands in a position totally different from that of ordinary religion. It does not put forward these great truths merely on the authority of some sacred book of long ago; in speaking of these subjects it is not dealing with pious opinions , or metaphysical speculations, but with solid, definite facts, as real and as close to us as the air we breathe or the houses we live in facts of which many among us have constant experience facts among which lies the daily work of some of our students, as will presently be seen.

Among the beautiful conceptions which Theosophy has restored to us stands pre-eminent that of the great helpful agencies of nature. The belief in these has been world-wide from the earliest dawn of history and is universal even now outside the narrow domains of Protestantism, which has emptied and darkened the world for its votaries by its attempt to do away with the natural and perfectly true idea of intermediate agents and reduce everything to two factors of man and deity, a device whereby the conception of deity has been infinitely degraded, and man has remained un-helped.

A moment's thought will show that the ordinary view of providence, the conception of an erratic interference by the central power of the universe with the result of his own decrees would imply the introduction of partiality into the scheme, and therefore of the whole train of evils which must necessarily follow upon its heels. The Theosophical teaching, that a man can be thus specially helped only when his past actions have been such as to deserve this assistance, and that even then the help will be given through those who are comparatively near his own level, is free from this serious objection; and it furthermore brings back to us the older and far grander conception of an unbroken ladder of living beings extending down from the Logos Himself to the very dust beneath our feet.

In the East the existence of the invisible helpers has always been recognized, though the names given, and the characteristics attributed to them naturally vary in different countries; and even in Europe we have had the old Greek stories of the constant interference of the gods in human affairs, and the Roman legend that Castor and Pollux led the legions of the infant republic in the battle of Lake

Regillus. Nor did such a conception die out when the classical period ended, for these stories have their legitimate successors in medieval tales of saints who appeared at critical moments and turned the fortune of war in favor of the Christian hosts, or of guardian angels who sometimes stepped in and saved a pious traveler from what would otherwise have been certain destruction.

— — —

CHAPTER II

Some Modern Instances

Even in this incredulous age, and amidst the full whirl of our nineteenth-century civilization, in spite of the dogmatism of our science and the deadly dullness of our Protestantism, instances of intervention inexplicable from the materialistic standpoint may still be found by anyone who will take the trouble to look for them; and in order to demonstrate this to the reader I will briefly epitomize a few of the examples given in one or other of the recent collections of such stories, adding thereto one or two that have come within my own notice.

One very remarkable feature of these more recent examples is that the intervention seems nearly always to have been directed towards the helping or saving of children.

An interesting case which occurred in London only a few years ago was connected with the preservation of a child's life in the midst of a terrible fire, which broke out in a street near Holborn, and entirely destroyed two of the houses there. The flames had obtained such hold before they were discovered that the firemen were unable to save the houses, but they succeeded in rescuing all the inmates except two - an old woman who was suffocated by the smoke before they could reach her, and a child about five years old, whose presence in the house had been forgotten in the hurry and excitement of the moment.

The mother of the child, it seems, was a friend or relative of the landlady of the house and had left the little creature in her charge for the night, because she was herself obliged to go down to Colchester on business. It was not until everyone else had been rescued, and the whole house was wrapped in flame, that the landlady remembered with a terrible pang the trust that had been confided to her. It seemed hopeless then to attempt to get at the garret where the child had been put to bed, but one of the firemen heroically resolved to make the desperate effort and after receiving minute directions as to the exact situation of the room, plunged in among the smoke and flame.

He found the child and brought him forth entirely unharmed; but when he rejoined his comrades, he had a very singular story to tell. He declared that when he reached the room he found it in flames, and most of the floor already fallen; but the fire had curved round the room towards the window in an unnatural and unaccountable manner, the like of which in all his experience he had never seen before, so that the corner in which the child lay was wholly untouched, although the very rafters of the fragment of floor on which his little crib stood were half burnt away. The child was naturally very much terrified, but the fireman distinctly and repeatedly declared that as at great risk he made his way towards him he saw a form like an angel - here his exact words are given - something "all gloriously white and silvery, bending over the bed and smoothing down the counterpane." He could not possibly have been mistaken about it, he said, for it was visible in a glare of light for some moments, and in fact disappeared only when he was within a few feet of it.

Another curious feature of this story is that the child's mother found herself unable to sleep that night down in Colchester but was constantly harassed by a strong feeling that something was wrong with her child, insomuch that at last she was compelled to rise and spend some time in earnest prayer that the little one might be protected from the danger which she instinctively felt to be hanging over him.

The intervention was thus evidently what a Christian would call an answer to a prayer; a Theosophist, putting the same idea in more scientific phraseology, would say that her intense outpouring of love constituted a force which one of our visible helpers was able to use for the rescue of her child from a terrible death.

A remarkable case in which children were abnormally protected occurred on the banks of the Thames near Maidenhead a few years earlier than our last example. This time the danger from which they were saved arose not from fire but from water. Three little ones, who lived, if I recollect rightly, in or near the village of Shottesbrook, were taken out for a walk along the towing-path by their nurse. They rushed suddenly round a corner upon a horse which was drawing a barge, and in the confusion two of them got on the wrong side of the towrope and were thrown into the water.

The boatman, who saw the accident, sprang forward to try to save them, and he noticed that they were floating high in the water "in quite an unnatural way, like," as he said, and moving quietly towards the bank. This was all that he and the nurse saw, but the children each declared that "a beautiful person, all white and shining," stood beside them in the water, held them up and guided them to the shore. Nor was their story without corroboration, for the bargeman's little daughter, who ran up from the cabin when she heard the screams of the nurse, also affirmed that she saw a lovely lady in the water dragging the two children to the bank.

Without fuller particulars than the story gives us, it is impossible to say with certainty from what class of helpers this "angel" was drawn; but the probabilities are in favour of its having been a developed human being functioning in the astral body, as will be seen when later on we deal with this subject from the other side, as it were from the point of view of the helpers rather than the helped.

A case in which the agency is somewhat more definitely distinguishable is related by the well-known clergyman, Dr John Mason Neale. He states that a man who had recently lost his wife was on a visit with his little children at the country house of a friend. It was an old, rambling mansion, and in the lower part of it there were long, dark passages, in which the children played about with great delight. But presently they came upstairs very gravely, and two of them related that as they were running down one of these passages they were met by their mother, who told them to go back again, and then disappeared. Investigation revealed the fact that if the children had run but a few steps farther they would have fallen down a deep uncovered well which yawned full in their path, so that the apparition of their mother had saved them from almost certain death.

In this instance there seems no reason to doubt that the mother herself was still keeping a loving watch over her children from the astral plane, and that (as has happened in some other cases) her intense desire to warn them of the danger into which they were so heedlessly rushing gave her the power to make herself visible and audible to them for the moment - or perhaps merely to impress their minds with the idea that they saw and heard her. It is possible, of course, that the helper may have been someone else, who took the familiar form of the mother in order not to alarm the children; but the simplest hypothesis is to attribute the intervention to the action of the ever-wakeful motherlove itself, undimmed by the passage through the gates of death.

This motherlove, being one of the holiest and most unselfish of human feelings, is also one of the most persistent on higher planes. Not only does the mother who finds herself upon the lower levels of the astral plane, and consequently still within touch of the earth, maintain her interest in and her care for her children as long as she is able to see them; even after her entry into the heaven world these little ones are still the most prominent objects in her thought, and the wealth of love that she lavishes upon the images which she there makes of them is a great outpouring of spiritual force which flows down upon her offspring who are still struggling in this lower world, and surrounds them with living centers of beneficent energy which may not inaptly be described as veritable guardian angels. An illustration of this will be found in the sixth of our Theosophical manuals, page 38.

Not long ago the little daughter of one of our English bishops was out walking with her mother in the town where they lived, and in running heedlessly across a street the child was knocked down by the horses of a carriage which came quickly upon her round a corner. Seeing her among the horses' feet, the mother rushed forward, expecting to find her very badly injured, but she sprang up quite merrily, saying, "Oh, mamma, I am not at all hurt, for something all in white kept the horses from treading upon me, and told me not to be afraid."

A case which occurred in Buckinghamshire, somewhere in the neighborhood of Burnham Beeches, is remarkable on account of the length of time through which the physical manifestation of the succoring agency seems to have maintained itself. It will have been seen that in the instances hitherto given the intervention was a matter of but a few moments, whereas in this a phenomenon was produced which appears to have persisted for more than half an hour.

Two of the little children of a small farmer were left to amuse themselves while their parents and their entire household were engaged in the work of harvesting. The little ones started for a walk in the woods, wandered far from home, and then managed to lose their way. When the weary parents returned at dusk it was discovered that the children were missing, and after enquiring at some of the neighbours' houses the father sent servants and labourers in various directions to seek for them.

Their efforts were, however, unsuccessful, and their shouts unanswered; and they had reassembled at the farm in a somewhat despondent frame of mind, when they all saw a curious light, some distance away moving slowly across some fields towards the road. It was described as a large globular mass of rich golden glow, quite unlike ordinary lamplight; and as it drew nearer it was seen that the two missing children were walking steadily along in the midst of it. The father and some others immediately set off running towards it; the appearance persisted until they were close to it, but just as they grasped the children it vanished, leaving them in the darkness.

The children's story was that after night came on, they had wandered about crying in the woods for some time and had at last lain down under a tree to sleep. They had been roused, they said, by a beautiful lady with a lamp, who took them by the hand and led them home; when they questioned her, she smiled at them, but never spoke a word. To this strange tale they both steadily adhered, nor was it possible in any way to shake their faith in what they had seen. It is noteworthy, however, that though all presents saw the light, and noticed that it lit up the trees and hedges which came within its sphere precisely as an ordinary light would, yet the form of the lady was visible to none but the children.

— — —

CHAPTER III

A Personal Experience

All the above stories are comparatively well known, and may be found in some of the books which contain collections of such accounts most of them in Dr Lee's More *Glimpses of the World Unseen*; but the two instances which I am now about to give have never been in print before, and both occurred within the last ten years - one to myself, and the other to a very dear friend of mine, a prominent member of the Theosophical Society, whose accuracy of observation is beyond all shadow of doubt.

My own story is a simple one enough, though not unimportant to me since the interposition undoubtedly saved my life. I was walking one exceedingly wet and stormy night down a quiet back street near Westbourne Grove, struggling with scant success to hold up an umbrella against the savage gusts of wind that threatened every moment to tear it from my grasp, and trying as I laboured along to think out the details of some work upon which I was just then engaged.

With startling suddenness, a voice which I know well, the voice of an Indian teacher cried in my ear "Spring back!" and in mechanical obedience I started violently backwards almost before I had time to think. As I did so my umbrella, which had swung forward with the sudden movement, was struck from my hand and a huge metal chimney pot crashed upon the pavement less than a yard in front of my face. The great weight of this article, and the tremendous force with which it fell, make it absolutely certain that but for the warning voice I should have been killed on the spot; yet the street was empty, and the voice was that of one whom I knew to be seven thousand miles away from me, as far as the physical body was concerned.

Nor was this the only occasion upon which I received assistance of this supernormal kind, for in early life, long before the foundation of the Theosophical Society, the apparition of a dear one who had recently died prevented me from committing what I now see would have been a serious crime, although by the light of such knowledge as I then had it appeared not only a justifiable but even a laudable act of retaliation. Again, at a later date, though still before the foundation of this Society, a warning conveyed to me from a higher plane amid most impressive surroundings enabled me to prevent another man from entering upon a course which I now know would have ended disastrously, though I had no reason to suppose so at the time. So, it will be seen that I have a certain amount of personal experience to strengthen my belief in the doctrine of invisible helpers, even apart from my knowledge of the help that is constantly being given at the present time.

The other case is a very much more striking one. One of our members, who gives me permission to publish her story, but does not wish her name mentioned, once found herself in very serious physical peril. Owing to circumstances which need not be detailed here, she was in the very center of a dangerous street fracas, and seeing several men struck down and evidently badly hurt close to her, was in momentary expectation of a similar fate, since escape from the crush seemed quite impossible.

Suddenly she experienced a curious sensation of being whirled out of the crowd and found herself standing quite uninjured and entirely alone in a small bye-street parallel with the one in which the disturbance had taken place. She still heard the noise of the struggle, and while she stood wondering what on earth had happened to her, two or three men who had escaped from the crowd came running round the corner of the street, and on seeing her expressed great astonishment and pleasure, saying that when the brave lady so suddenly disappeared from the midst of the fight, they had felt certain that she had been struck down.

At the time no sort of explanation was forthcoming, and she returned home in a very mystified condition; but when at a later period she mentioned this strange occurrence to Madame Blavatsky she was informed that, her karma being such as to enable her to be saved from her exceedingly dangerous position, one of the Masters had specially sent someone to protect her in view of the fact that her life was needed for the work.

Nevertheless, the case remains a very extraordinary one, both with regard to the great amount of power exercised and the unusually public nature of its manifestation. It is not difficult to imagine the *modus operandi*; she must have been lifted bodily over the intervening block of houses, and simply set down in the next street; but since her physical body was not visible floating in the air, it is also evident that a veil of some sort (probably of etheric matter) must have been thrown round her while in transit.

If it be objected that whatever can hide physical matter must itself be physical, and therefore visible, it may be replied that by a process familiar to all occult students it is possible to bend rays of light (which, under all conditions at present known to science, travel only in straight lines unless refracted) so that after passing round an object they may resume exactly their former course; and it will at once be seen that if this were done such an object would to all physical eyes be absolutely invisible until the rays were allowed to resume their normal course. I am fully aware that this one statement alone is sufficient to brand any remarks as nonsense in the eyes of the scientist of the present day, but I cannot help that; I am merely stating a possibility in nature which the science of the future will no doubt one day discover, and for those who are not students of occultism the remark must wait until then for its justification.

The process, as I say, is comprehensible enough to anyone who understands a little about the more occult forces of nature; but the phenomenon still remains an exceedingly dramatic one, while the name of the heroine of the story, were I permitted to give it, would be a guarantee of its accuracy to all my readers.

Another recent instance of interposition, less striking, perhaps, but entirely successful, has been reported to me since the publication of the first edition of this book. A lady, being obliged

to undertake a long railway journey alone, had taken the precaution to secure an empty compartment; but just as the train was leaving the station, a man of forbidding and villainous appearance sprang in and seated himself at the other end of the carriage. The lady was much alarmed thus, to be left alone with so doubtful a character, but it was too late to call for help, so she sat still and commended herself earnestly to the care of her patron saint.

Soon her fears were redoubled, for the man arose and turned toward her with an evil grin, but he had hardly taken one step when he started back with a look of the most intense astonishment and terror. Following the direction of his glance, she was startled to see a gentleman seated directly opposite to her, gazing quietly but firmly at the baffled robber, a gentleman who certainly could not have entered the carriage by any ordinary means. Too much awed to speak, she watched him as though fascinated for a full half-hour; he uttered no word, and did not even look at her, but kept his eyes steadily upon the villain, who cowered trembling in the furthest corner of the compartment. The moment that the train reached the next station, and even before it came to a standstill, the would-be thief tore open the door and sprang hurriedly out. The lady, deeply thankful to be rid of him, turned to express her gratitude to the gentleman, but found only an empty seat, though it would have been impossible for any physical body to have left the carriage in the time.

The materialization was in this case maintained for a longer period than usual, but on the other hand it expended no force in action of any kind, nor indeed was it necessary that it should do so, as its mere appearance was sufficient to effect its purpose.

But these stories, all referring as they do to what would commonly be called angelic intervention, illustrate only one small part of the activities of our invisible helpers. Before, however, we can profitably consider the other departments of their work it will be well that we should have clearly in our minds the various classes of entities to which it is possible that these helpers may belong. Let that, then, be the portion of our subject to be next treated.

— — —

CHAPTER IV

The Helpers

Help, then, may be given by several of the many classes of inhabitants of the astral plane. It may come from devas, from nature-spirits, or from those whom we call dead, as well as from those who function consciously upon the astral plane during life chiefly the adepts and their pupils. But if we examine the matter a little more closely, we shall see that though all the classes mentioned may, and sometimes do, take a part in this work, yet their shares in it are so unequal that it is practically left almost entirely to one class.

The very fact that so much of this work of helping has to be done either upon or from the astral plane goes far in itself towards explaining this. To anyone who has even a faint idea of what the powers at the command of an adept really are, it will be at once obvious that for him to work upon the astral plane would be a far greater waste of energy than for our leading physicians or scientists to spend their time in breaking stones upon the road.

The work of the adept lies in higher regions chiefly upon the arûpa levels of the devachanic plane or heaven-world, where he may direct his energies to the influencing of the true individuality of man, and not the mere personality which is all that can be reached in the astral or physical world. The strength which he puts forth in that more exalted realm produces results greater, more far-reaching and more lasting than any which can be attained by the expenditure of even ten times the force down here; and the work up there is such as he alone can fully accomplish, while that on lower planes may be at any rate to some extent achieved by whose feet are yet upon the earlier steps of the great stairway which will one day lead them to the position where he stands.

The same remarks apply also in the case of the devas. Belonging as they do to a higher kingdom of nature than ours, their work seems for the most part entirely unconnected with humanity; and even those of their orders and there are some such, which do sometimes respond to our higher yearnings or appeals, do so on the mental plane rather than on the physical or astral, and more frequently in the periods between our incarnations than during our earthly lives.

It may be remembered that some instances of such help were observed in the course of investigations into the subdivisions of the devachanic plane which were undertaken when the Theosophical manual on the subject was in preparation. In one case a deva was found teaching the most wonderful celestial music to a chorister; and in another one of a different class was giving instruction and guidance to an astronomer who was seeking to comprehend the form and structure of the universe.

These two were but examples of many instances in which the great deva kingdom was found to be helping onward the evolution and responding to the higher aspirations of man after death; and there are methods by which, even during earth-life, these great ones may be approached, and an infinity of knowledge acquired from them, though even then such intercourse is gained rather by rising to their plane than by invoking them to descend to ours.

In the ordinary events of our physical life the deva very rarely interferes indeed, he is so fully occupied with the far grander work of his own plane that he is probably scarcely conscious of this and though it may occasionally happen that he becomes aware of some human sorrow or difficulty which excites his pity and moves him to endeavour to help in some way, his wider vision undoubtedly recognizes that at the present stage of evolution such interpositions would in the vast majority of cases be productive of infinitely more harm than good.

There was indubitably a period in the past - in the infancy of the human race, when it was much more largely assisted from outside than is at present the case. At the time when all its Buddhas and Manus, and even its more ordinary leaders and teachers, were drawn either from the ranks of the deva evolution or from the perfected humanity of a more advanced planet, any such assistance as we are considering in this treatise must also have been given by these exalted beings. But as man progresses, he becomes himself qualified to act as a helper, first on the physical plane and then on higher levels; and we have now reached a stage at which humanity ought to be able to provide, and to some slight extent does provide, invisible helpers for itself, thus setting free for still more useful and elevated work those beings who are capable of it.

It becomes obvious then that such assistance as that to which we are here referring may most fitly be given by men and women at a particular stage of their evolution; not by the adepts, since they are capable of doing far grander and more widely useful work, and not by the ordinary person of no special spiritual development, for he would be unable to be of any use. Just as these considerations would lead us to expect, we find that this work of helping on the astral and lower mental planes is chiefly in the hands of the pupils of the master's men who, though yet far from the attainment of adept ship, have evolved themselves to the extent of being able to function consciously upon the planes in question.

Some of these have taken the further step of completing the links between the physical consciousness and that of the higher levels, and they therefore have the undoubted advantage of recollecting in waking life what they have done and what they have learnt in those other worlds; but there are my others who, though as yet unable to carry their consciousness through unbroken, are nevertheless by no means wasting the hours when they think they are asleep, but spending them in noble and unselfish labour for their fellow-men.

What this labour is we will proceed to consider, but before we enter upon that part of the subject, we will refer to an objection which is very frequently brought forward with regard to such work, and we will also dispose of the comparatively rare cases in which the agents are either nature-spirits or men who have cast off the physical body.

People whose grasp of Theosophical ideas is as yet imperfect are often in doubt as to whether it is allowable for them to try to help someone whom they find in sorrow or difficulty, lest they should interfere with the fate which has been decreed for him by the absolute justice of the eternal law of karma. "The man is in his present position," they say in effect, "because he has deserved it; he is now working out the perfectly natural result of some evil which he has committed in the past; what right have I to interfere with the action of the great cosmic law by trying to ameliorate his condition, either on the astral plane or the physical.

Now the good people who make such suggestions are really, however unconsciously to themselves, exhibiting the most colossal conceit, for their position implies two astounding assumptions; first, that they know exactly what another man's karma has been, and how long it has decreed that his sufferings shall last; and secondly, that they, the insects of a day could absolutely override the cosmic law and prevent the due working-out of karma by any action of theirs. We may be well assured that the great karmic deities are perfectly well able to manage their business without our assistance, and we need have no fear that any steps we may take can by any possibility cause them the slightest difficulty or uneasiness.

If a man's karma is such that he cannot be helped, then all our well-meant efforts in that direction will fail, though we shall nevertheless have gained good karma for ourselves by making them. What the man's karma has been is no business of ours; our duty is to give help to the utmost of our power, and our right is only to the act; the result is in other and higher hands. How can we tell how a man's account stands? For all we know he may just have exhausted his evil karma, and be at this moment at the very point where a helping hand is needed to give relief and raise him out of his trouble or depression; why should not we have the pleasure and privilege of doing that good deed as well as another? If we *can* help him, then that fact of itself shows that he has deserved to be helped; but we can never know unless we try. In any case the law of karma will take care of itself, and we need not trouble ourselves about it.

The cases in which assistance is given to mankind by nature-spirits are few. The majority of such creatures shun the haunts of man, and retire before him, disliking his emanations and the perpetual bustle and unrest which he creates all around him. Also, except some of their higher orders, they are generally inconsequent and thoughtless more like happy children at play under exceedingly favorable physical conditions than like grave and responsible entities. Still, it sometimes happens that one of them will become attached to a human being and do him many a good turn; but at the present stage of its evolution this department of nature cannot be relied upon for anything like steady co-operation in the work of invisible helpers. For a fuller account of the nature-spirits the reader is referred to the fifth of our Theosophical manuals.

Again, help is sometimes given by those recently departed - those who are still lingering on the astral plane, and still in close touch with earthly affairs, as (probably) in the above-mentioned case of the mother who saved her children from falling down a well. But it will readily be seen that the amount of such help available must naturally be exceedingly limited. The more unselfish and helpful a person is, the less likely is he to be found after death lingering in full consciousness on the lower levels of the astral plane, from which the earth is most readily accessible. In any case, unless he were an exceptionally bad man, his stay within the realm whence alone any interference would be possible would be comparatively short; and although from the heaven-world he may still shed benign influence upon those whom he has loved on earth, it will usually be rather of the nature of a general benediction than a force capable of bringing about definite results in a specific case, such as those which we have been considering.

Again, many of the departed who wish to help those whom they left behind, find themselves quite unable to influence them in any way, since to work from one plane upon an entity on another requires either very great sensitiveness on the part of that entity, or a certain amount of knowledge and skill on the part of the operator. Therefore, although instances of apparitions shortly after death are by no means uncommon, it is rare to find one in which the departed person has really done anything useful or succeeded in impressing what he wished upon the friend or relation whom he visited. There are such cases, of course - a good many of them when we come to put them all together; but they are not numerous compared to the great number of ghosts who have succeeded in showing themselves. So that but little help is usually given by the dead - indeed, as will presently be explained, it is far more common for them to be themselves in need of assistance than to be able to accord it to others.

At present, therefore, the main bulk of the work which has to be done along these lines falls to the share of those living persons who are able to function consciously on the astral plane

— — —

CHAPTER V

The Reality of Superphysical Life

It seems difficult for those who are accustomed only to the ordinary and somewhat materialistic lines of thought of the nineteenth century, to believe in and realize fully a condition of perfect consciousness apart from the physical body. Every Christian, at any rate, is bound by the very foundations of his creed to believe that he possesses a soul; but if you suggest to him the possibility that that soul may be a sufficiently real thing to become visible under certain conditions apart from the body either during life or after death, the chances are ten to one that he will scornfully tell you that he does not believe in ghosts, and that such an idea is nothing but an anachronistic survival of an exploded medieval superstition.

If, therefore, we are at all to comprehend the work of the band of invisible helpers, and perchance ourselves to learn to assist in it, we must shake ourselves free from the trammels of contemporary thought on these subjects, and endeavour to grasp the great truth (now a demonstrated fact to many among us) that the physical body is in simple truth nothing but a vehicle or vesture of the real man. It is put off permanently at death, but it is also put off temporarily every night when we go to sleep indeed the process of falling asleep consists in this very action of the real man in his astral vehicle slipping out of the physical body.

Again, I repeat this is no mere hypothesis or ingenious supposition. There are many among us who are able to perform (and do perform every day of their lives) this elementary act of magic in full consciousness who pass from one plane to the other at will; and if that is clearly realized, it will become apparent how grotesquely absurd to them must appear the ordinary unreasoning assertion that such a thing is utterly impossible. It is like telling a man that it is impossible for him to fall asleep, and that if he thinks he has ever done so he is under a hallucination.

Now the man who has not yet developed the link between the astral and physical consciousness is unable to leave his denser body at will, or to recollect most of what happens to him while away from it; but the fact nevertheless remains that he leaves it every time he sleeps and may be seen by any trained clairvoyant either hovering over it or wandering about at a greater or less distance from it, as the case may be.

The entirely undeveloped person usually floats close above his physical body, scarcely less asleep than it is, and comparatively shapeless and inchoate, and it is found that he cannot be drawn away from the immediate neighbour hood of that physical body without causing serious discomfort which would in fact awaken it. As the man evolves, however, his astral body grows more definite and more conscious, and so becomes a fitter vehicle for him. In the case of the majority of intelligent and cultured people the degree of consciousness is already very considerable, and a man who is at all spiritually developed is as fully himself in that vehicle as in this denser body.

But though he may be fully conscious on the astral plane during sleep, and able to move about on it freely if he wishes to do so, it does not yet follow that he is ready to join the band of helpers. Most people at this stage are so wrapped up in their own train of thought usually a continuation of some line taken up in waking hours that they are like a man in a brown study, so much absorbed as to be practically entirely heedless of all that is going on about them. And in many ways, it is well that this is so, for there is much upon the astral plane which might be unnerving and terrifying to one who had not the courage born of full knowledge as to the real nature of all that he would see.

Sometimes a man gradually rouses himself out of this condition - wakes up to the astral world around him, as it were; but more often he remains in that state until someone who is already active there takes him in hand and wakens him. This is, however, not a responsibility to be lightly undertaken, for while it is comparatively easy thus to wake a man up on the astral plane, it is practically impossible, except by a most undesirable exercise of mesmeric influence, to put him to sleep again. So that before a member of the band of workers will thus awaken a dreamer, he must fully satisfy himself that the man's disposition is such that he will make good use of the additional powers that will then be put into his hands, and also that his knowledge and his courage are sufficient to make it reasonably certain that no harm will come to him as a result of the action.

Such awakening so performed will put a man in a position to join if he will the band of those who help mankind. But it must be clearly understood that this does not necessarily or even usually bring with it the power of remembering in the waking consciousness anything which has been done. That capacity has to be attained by the man for himself, and in most cases, it does not come for years afterwards perhaps not even in the same life. But happily, this lack of memory in the body in no way impedes the work out of the body; so that, except for the satisfaction to a man of knowing during his waking hours upon what work he has been engaged during his sleep, it is not a matter of importance. What really matters is that the work should be done not that we should remember who did it.

— — —

CHAPTER VI

A Timely Intervention

Varied as is this work on the astral plane, it is all directed to one great end, the furtherance, in however humble a degree, of the processes of evolution. Occasionally it is connected with the development of the lower kingdoms, which it is possible slightly to accelerate under certain conditions. A duty towards these lower kingdoms, elemental as well as animal and vegetable, is distinctly recognized by our adept leaders, since it is in some cases only through connection with or use by man that their progress takes place.

But naturally by far the largest and most important part of the work is connected with humanity in some way or other. The services rendered are of many and various kinds, but chiefly concerned with man's spiritual development, such physical interventions as are recounted in the earlier part of this book being exceedingly rare. They do, however, occasionally take place, and though it is my wish to emphasize rather the possibility of extending mental and moral help to our fellow-men, it will perhaps be well to give two or three instances in which friends personally known to me have rendered physical assistance to those in sore need of it, in order that it may be seen how these examples from the experience of the helpers gear in with the accounts given by those who have received the supernormal aid - such stories, I mean, as those which are to be found in the literature of so-called "supernatural occurrences."

In the course of the recent rebellion in Matabeleland one of our members was sent upon an errand of mercy which may serve as an illustration of the way in which help upon this lower plane has occasionally been given. It seems that one night a certain farmer and his family in that country were sleeping tranquilly in fancied security, quite unaware that only a few miles away relentless hordes of savage foes were lying in ambush maturing fiendish plots of murder and rapine. Our member's business was in some way or other to arouse the sleeping family to a sense of the terrible danger which so unexpectedly menaced them, and she found this by no means an easy matter.

An attempt to impress the idea of imminent peril upon the brain of the farmer failed utterly, and as the urgency of the case seemed to demand strong measures, our friend decided to materialize herself sufficiently to shake the housewife by the shoulder and adjure her to get up and look about her. The moment she saw that she had been successful in attracting attention she vanished, and the farmer's wife has never from that day to this been able to find out *which* of her neighbours it was who roused her so opportunely, and thus saved the lives of the entire family, who but for this mysterious intervention would undoubtedly have been massacred in their beds half an hour later; nor can she even now understand how this friend in need contrived to make her way in, when all the windows and doors were found so securely barred.

Being this abruptly awakened, the housewife was half inclined to consider the warning a mere dream; however, she arose and looked around just to see that all was right, and fortunate it was that she did so, for though she found nothing amiss indoors she had no sooner thrown open a shutter than she saw the sky red with a distant conflagration. She at once roused her husband and the rest of the family and owing to this timely notice they were able to escape to a place of concealment near at hand just before the arrival of the horde of savages, who destroyed the house and ravaged the fields indeed, but were disappointed of the human prey which they had expected. The feelings of the rescuer may be imagined when she read in the newspaper some time afterwards an account of the providential deliverance of this family.

— — —

CHAPTER VII

The "Angel Story."

Another instance of intervention on the physical plane which occurred a short time ago makes a very beautiful little story, though this time only one life was saved. It needs, however, a few words of preliminary explanation. Among our band of helpers here in Europe are two who were brothers long ago in ancient Egypt and are still warmly attached to one another. In this present incarnation there is a wide difference in age between them, one being advanced in middle life, while the other was at that time a mere child in the physical body, though an ego of considerable advancement and promise. Naturally it falls to the lot of the elder to train and guide the younger in the occult work to which they are so heartily devoted, and as both are fully conscious and active on the astral plane, they spend most of the time during which their grosser bodies are asleep in labouring together under the direction of their common Master and giving to both living and dead such help as is within their power.

I will quote the story of the particular incident which I wish to relate from a letter written by the elder of the two helpers immediately after its occurrence, as the description there given is more vivid and picturesque than any account in the third person could possibly be.

"We were going about quite other business, when Cyril suddenly cried, 'What's that?' for we heard a terrible scream of pain or fright. In a moment we were on the spot and found that a boy of about eleven or twelve had fallen over a cliff on to some rocks below and was very badly hurt. He had broken a leg and an arm, poor fellow, but what was still worse was a dreadful cut in the thigh, from which blood was pouring in a torrent. Cyril cried, 'Let us help him quick, or he'll die!'

"In emergencies of this kind one has to think quickly. There were clearly two things to be done; that bleeding must be stopped, and physical help must be procured. I was obliged to materialize either Cyril or myself, for we wanted physical hands at once to tie a bandage, and besides it seemed better that the poor boy should *see* someone standing by him in his trouble. I felt that while undoubtedly, he would be more at home with Cyril than with me, I should probably be more readily able to procure help than Cyril would, so the division of labour was obvious.

"The plan worked capitally. I materialized Cyril instantly (he does not know yet how to do it for himself) and told him to take the boy's neckerchief and tie it round the thigh and twist a stick through it. 'Won't it hurt him terribly? said Cyril; but he *did* it, and the blood stopped flowing. The injured boy seemed half unconscious, and could scarcely speak, but he looked up at the shining little form bending so anxiously over him, and asked, 'Be you an angel, master?' Cyril smiled so prettily, and replied, 'No, I'm only a boy, but I've come to help you;' and then I left him to comfort the sufferer while I rushed off to the boy's mother, who lived about a mile away.

"The trouble I had to force into that woman's head the conviction that something was wrong, and that she must go and see about it, you would never believe; but at last, she threw down the pan she was cleaning, and said aloud, 'Well, I don't know what's come over me, but I must go and find the boy.' When she once started, I was able to guide her without much difficulty, though at the time I was holding Cyril together by willpower, lest the poor child's angel should suddenly vanish from before his eyes.

"You see, when you materialize a form, you are changing matter from its natural state into another - temporarily opposing the cosmic will, as it were; and if you take your mind off it for one half-second, back it flies into its original condition like a flash of lightning. So, I could not give more than half my attention to that woman, but still I got her along somehow, and as soon as she came round the corner of the cliff, I let Cyril disappear; but she had seen him, and now that village has one of the best-attested stories of angelic intervention on record!

"The accident happened in the early morning and the same evening I looked in (astrally) upon the family to see how matters were going on. The poor boy's leg and arm had been set, and the great cut bandaged, and he lay in bed looking very pale and weak, but evidently going to recover in time. The mother had a couple of neighbours in, and was telling them the story; and a curious tale it sounded to one who knew the real facts.

"She explained, in very many words, how she couldn't tell what it was, but something came over her all in a minute like, making her feel something had happened to the boy, and she must go out and see after him; how at first she thought it was nonsense, and tried to throw off the feeling, 'but it wasn't no use, she just had to go.' She told how she didn't know what made her go round by that cliff more than any other way, but it just happened so, and as she turned round the corner there she saw him lying propped up against a rock, and kneeling beside him was the 'beautifullest child ever she saw, dressed all in white and shining, with rosy cheeks and lovely brown eyes;' and how he smiled at her 'so heavenly like,' and then all in a moment he was not there, and at first she was so startled she didn't know what to think; and then all at once she felt what it was, and fell on her knees and thanked God for sending one of his angels to help her poor boy.

"Then she told how when she lifted him to carry him home she wanted to take off the handkerchief that was cutting into his poor leg so, but he would not let her, because he said the angel had tied it and said he was not to touch it; and how when she told the doctor this afterwards he explained to her that if she had unfastened it the boy would certainly have died.

"Then she repeated the boy's part of the tale, how the moment after he fell this lovely little angel came to him (he knew it was an angel because he knew there had been nobody in sight for half a mile round when he was at the top of the cliff just before only he could not understand why it hadn't any wings, and why it said it was only a boy) how it lifted him against the rock and tied up his leg, and then began to talk to him and tell him he need not be frightened, because somebody was gone to fetch mother, and she would be there directly; how it kissed him and tried to make him comfortable, and how its soft, warm, little hand held his all the time, while it told him strange, beautiful stories which he could not clearly remember, but he knew they were very good, because he had almost forgotten he was hurt until he saw his mother coming; and how then it assured him he would soon be well again, and smiled and squeezed his hand, and then somehow it was gone.

"Since then, there has been quite a religious revival in that village! Their minister has told them that so signal an interposition of divine providence must have been meant as a sign to them, to rebuke scoffers and to prove the truth of holy scripture and of the Christian religion and nobody seems to see the colossal conceit involved in such an astonishing proposition.

"But the effect on the boy had been undoubtedly good, morally as well as physically; by all accounts he was a careless enough young scamp before, but now he feels 'his angel' may be near him at any time, and he will never do or say anything rough or coarse or angry, lest it should see or hear. The one great desire of his life is that someday he may see It again, and he knows that when he dies its lovely face will be the first to greet him on the other side.

A beautiful and pathetic little story, truly. The moral dawn from the occurrence by the village and its minister is perhaps somewhat of a *non sequitur*; yet the testimony to the existence of at least something beyond this material plane must surely do the people more good than harm, and after all the mother's conclusion from what she saw was a perfectly correct one, though more accurate knowledge would probably have led her to express it a little differently.

An interesting fact afterwards discovered by the investigations of the writer of the letter throws a curious sidelight upon the reasons underlying such incidents. It was found that the two boys had met before, and that some thousands of years ago the one who fell from the cliff had been the slave of the other, and had once saved his young master's life at the risk of his own, and had been liberated in consequence; and now, long afterwards, the master not only repays the debt in kind, but also gives his former slave a high ideal and an inducement to morality of life which will probably change the whole course of his future evolution. So true is it that no good deed ever goes unrewarded by karma, however tardy it may seem in its action that

Though the mills of God grind slowly

Yet they grind exceeding small,

Though with patience stands

He waiting,

With exactness grinds He all.

CHAPTER VIII

The Story Of A Fire

Another piece of work done by the same boy Cyril furnishes an almost exact parallel to some of the stories from the books which I have given in earlier pages. He and his older friend, it seems, were passing along in the prosecution of their usual work one night, when they noticed the fierce glare of a big fire below them, and promptly dived down to see if they could be of any use.

It was a great hotel which was in flames, a huge caravanserai on the edge of a great lake. The house, many stories in height, formed three sides of a square round a sort of garden, planted with trees and flowers, while the lake formed the fourth side. The two wings ran right down to the lake, the big bay windows which terminated them almost projecting over the water, so as to leave only quite a narrow passageway under them at the two sides.

The front and wings were built round inside wells, which also contained the lattice-work shafts of the lifts, so that when once the fire broke out, it spread with almost incredible rapidity, and before our friends saw it on their astral journey all the middle floors in each of the three great blocks were in flames. Fortunately, the inmates except one little boy had already been rescued, though some of them had sustained very serious burns and other injuries.

This little fellow had been forgotten in one of the upper rooms of the left wing, for his parents were out at a ball, and knew nothing of the fire, while naturally enough no one else thought of the lad till it was far too late. The fire had gained such a hold on the middle floors of that wing that nothing could have been done, even if anyone had remembered him, as his room faced on to the inner garden which has been mentioned, so that he was completely cut off from all outside help. Besides, he was not even aware of his danger, for the dense, suffocating smoke had so gradually filled the room that his sleep had grown deeper and deeper, till he was all but stupefied.

In this state he was discovered by Cyril, who seems to be specially attracted towards children in need or danger. He first tried to make some of the people remember the boy, but in vain; and in any case it seemed scarcely possible that they could have helped him, so that it was soon evident that this was merely a waste of time. The older helper then materialized, Cyril, as before, in the room, and set him to work to awaken and rouse up the more than half-stupefied child. After a good deal of difficulty this was accomplished to some extent, but the boy remained in a half-dazed, semi-conscious condition through all that followed, so that he needed to be pushed and pulled about, guided, and helped at every turn.

The two boys first crept out of the room into the central passage which ran through the wing, and then, finding that the smoke and the flames beginning to come through the floor made it impassable for a physical body, Cyril got the other boy back into the room again and out of the window on to a stone ledge, about a foot wide, which ran right along the block just below the windows. Along this he managed to guide his companion, half balancing himself on the extreme edge of the ledge, and half floating on air, but always placing himself outside of the other, so as to keep him from dizziness and prevent him from feeling afraid of a fall.

Towards the end of the block nearest the lake, in which direction the fire seemed less developed, they climbed in through an open window and again reached the passage, hoping to find the staircase at that end still passable. But it, too, was full of flame and smoke; so, they crawled back along the passage, Cyril advising his companion to keep his mouth close to the ground, till they reached the latticed cage of the lift running down the long well in the center of the block.

The lift of course was at the bottom, but they managed to clamber down the lattice work inside the cage till they stood on the roof of the elevator itself. Here they found themselves blocked, but luckily Cyril discovered a doorway opening from the cage of the lift on to a sort of *entresol* just above the ground floor. Through this they reached a passage, which they crossed, the little boy being half-stifled by the smoke; then they made their way through one of the rooms opposite, and finally, clambering out of the window, found themselves on the top of the veranda which ran along in front of the ground floor, between it and the garden.

There it was easy enough to swarm down one of the pillars and reach the garden itself; but even there the heat was intense, and the danger, when the walls should fall, very considerable. So, Cyril tried to conduct his charge round the end first of one, then of the other wing; but in both cases the flames had burst through, and the narrow, overhung passages were quite impassable. Finally, they took refuge in one of the pleasure boats which were moored to the steps of the quay at the side of the garden next the lake, and, casting loose, rowed out on to the water.

Cyril intended to row round past the burning wing and land the boy whom he had saved; but when they got some little way out, they fell in with a passing lake steamer, and were seen - for the whole scene was lit up by the glare of the burning hotel, till everything was as plain as in broad daylight. The steamer came alongside the boat to take them off; but instead of the two boys they had seen, the crew found only one for his older friend had promptly allowed Cyril to slip back into his astral form, dissipating the denser matter which had made for the time a material body, and he was therefore now invisible.

A careful search was made, of course, but no trace of the second boy could be found, and so it was concluded that he must have fallen overboard and been drowned just as they came alongside. The child who had been rescued fell into a dead faint as soon as he was safe on board, so they could get no information from him, and when he did recover, all he could say was that he had seen the other boy the moment before they came alongside, and then knew nothing more.

The steamer was bound down the lake to a place some two days' sail distant, and it was a week or so before the rescued boy could be restored to his parents, who of course thought that he had perished in the flames, for though an effort was made to impress on their minds the fact that their son had been saved, it was found impossible to convey the idea to them, so it may be imagined how great was the joy of the meeting.

The boy is still well and happy and is never weary of relating his wonderful adventure. Many a time he has regretted that the kind friend who saved him should have perished so mysteriously at the very moment when all the danger seemed over at last. Indeed, he has even ventured to suggest that perhaps he *didn't* perish after all that perhaps he was a fairy prince but of course this idea elicits nothing but tolerant smiles of superiority from his elders. The karmic link between him and his preserver has not yet been traced, but no doubt there must be one somewhere.

— — —

CHAPTER IX

Materialization And Repercussion

On meeting with a story such as this, students often enquire whether the invisible helper is perfectly safe amidst these scenes of deadly peril whether, for example, this boy who was materialized in order to save another from a burning house was not himself in some danger whether his physical body would not have suffered in any way by repercussion if his materialized form had passed through the flames, or fallen from the high ledge on the edge of which he walked so unconcernedly. In fact, since we know that in many cases the connection between a materialized form and a physical body is sufficiently close to produce repercussion, might it not have occurred in this case?

Now this subject of repercussion is an exceedingly abstruse and difficult one, and we are by no means yet in a position fully to explain its very remarkable phenomena; in order to understand the matter perfectly, it would probably be necessary to comprehend the laws of sympathetic vibration on more planes than one. Still, we do know by observation some of the conditions which permit its action, and some which definitely exclude it, and I think we are warranted in saying that it was absolutely impossible here.

To see why this is so we must first remember that there are at least three well-defined varieties of materialization, as anyone who has at all an extended experience of spiritualism will be aware. I am not concerned at the moment to enter upon any explanation as to how these three varieties are respectively produced but am merely stating the indubitable fact of their existence.

There is the materialization which, though tangible, is not visible to ordinary physical sight. Of this nature are the unseen hands which so often clasp one's arm or stroke one's face at a *seance*, which sometimes carry physical objects through the air or make raps upon the table though of course both these latter phenomena may easily be produced without a materialized hand at all.

There is the materialization which though visible is not tangible the spirit-form through which one's hand passed as through empty air. In some cases, this variety is obviously misty and impalpable, but in others its appearance is so entirely normal that its solidity is never doubted until someone endeavours to grasp it.

There is the perfect materialization which is both visible and tangible which not only bears the outward semblance of your departed friend but shakes you cordially by the hand with the very clasp that you know so well.

Now while there is a good deal of evidence to show that repercussion takes place under certain conditions in the case of this third kind of materialization., it is by no means so certain that it can occur with the first or second class. In the case of the boy-helper it is probable that the materialization would not be of the third type, since the greatest care is always taken not to expend more force than is absolutely necessary to produce whatever result may be required, and it is obvious that less energy would be used in the production of the more partial forms which we have called the first and second classes. The probability is that only the arm with which the boy held his little companion would be solid to the touch, and that the rest of his body, though looking perfectly natural, would have proved far less palpable if it had been tested.

But, apart from this probability, there is another point to be considered. When a full materialization takes place, whether the subject be living or dead, physical matter of some sort has to be gathered together for the purpose. At a spiritualistic *séance* this matter is obtained by drawing largely upon the etheric double of the medium - and sometimes even upon his physical body also, since cases are on record in which his weight has been very considerably decreased while manifestations of this character were taking place.

This method is employed by the directing entities of the *seance* simply because when an available medium is within reach it is very much the easiest way in which a materialization can be brought about; and the consequence is that the very closest connection is thus set up between that medium and the materialized body, so that the phenomenon which (although very imperfectly understanding it) we call repercussion, occurs in its clearest form. If, for example, the hands of the materialized body be rubbed with chalk, that chalk will afterwards be found on the hands of the medium, even though he may have been all the time carefully locked up in a cabinet under circumstances which absolutely preclude any suspicion of fraud. If any injury be inflicted upon the materialized form, that injury will be accurately reproduced upon the corresponding part of the medium's body: while sometimes food of which the spirit-form has partaken will be found to have passed into the body of the medium at least that happened in one case at any rate within my own experience.

It would be far otherwise, however, in the case which we have been describing. Cyril was thousands of miles from his sleeping physical body, and it would therefore be quite impossible for his friend to draw etheric matter from it, while the regulations under which all pupils of the great Masters of Wisdom perform their work of helping man would assuredly prevent him, even for the noblest purpose, from putting such a strain upon anyone else's body. Besides, it would be quite unnecessary, for the far less dangerous method invariably employed by the helpers when materialization seems desirable would be ready to his hand - the condensation from the circumambient ether, or even from the physical air, of such an amount of matter as may be requisite. This feat, though no doubt beyond the power of the average entity manifesting at a *seance*, presents no difficulty to a student of occult chemistry.

But mark the difference in the result obtained. In the case of the medium, we have a materialized form in the closest possible connection with the physical body, made out of its very substance, and therefore capable of producing all the phenomena of repercussion. In the case of the helper, we have indeed an exact reproduction of the physical body, but it is created by a mental effort out of matter entirely foreign to that body and is no more capable of acting upon it by repercussion than an ordinary marble statue of the man would be.

Thus, it is that a passage through the flames or a fall from a high window ledge would have had no terrors for the boy-helper, and that on another occasion a member of the band, though materialized, was able without any inconvenience to the physical body to go down in a sinking vessel.

In both the incidents of his work that have been described above, it will have been noticed that the boy Cyril was unable to materialize himself, and that the operation had to be performed for him by an older friend. One more of his experiences is worth relating, for it gives us a case in which by intensity of pity and determination of will he was able to show himself a case somewhat parallel to that previously related of the mother whose love enabled her somehow to manifest herself in order to save her children's lives.

Inexplicable as it may seem, there is no doubt whatever of the existence in nature of this stupendous power of will over matter of all planes, so that if only the power be great enough, practically *any* result may be produced by its direct action, without any knowledge or even thought, on the part of the man exercising that will as to how it is to do its work. We have had plenty of evidence that this power holds good in the case of materialization, although ordinarily it is an art which must be learnt just like any other. Assuredly an average man on the astral plane could no more materialize himself without having previously learnt how to do it than the average man on this plane could play the violin without having previously learnt it; but there are exceptional cases, as will be seen from the following narrative.

- - -

CHAPTER X

The Two Brothers

This story has been told by a pen of far greater dramatic capability than mine, and with a wealth of detail for which I have here no space, in *The Theosophical Review* of November 1897, page 229. To that account I would refer the reader, since my own description of the case will be a mere outline, as brief as is consistent with clearness. The names given are of course fictitious, but the incidents are related with scrupulous accuracy.

Our *dramatis personae* are two brothers, the sons of a country gentleman Lancelot, aged fourteen, and Walter, aged eleven very good boys of the ordinary healthy, manly type, like hundreds of others in this fair realm, with no obvious psychic qualifications of any sort, except the possession of a good deal of Celtic blood. Perhaps the most remarkable feature about them was the intensity of the affection that existed between them, for they were simply inseparable neither would go anywhere without the other, and the younger idolized the elder as only a younger boy can.

One unlucky day Lancelot was thrown from his pony and killed, and for Walter the world became empty. The child's grief was so real and terrible that he could neither eat not sleep, and his mother and nurse were at their wits' end as to what to do for him. He seemed deaf alike to persuasion and blame; when they told him that grief was wicked, and that his brother was in heaven, he simply answered that he could not be certain of that, and that even if it were true, he knew that Lancelot could no more be happy in heaven without him than he could on earth without Lancelot.

Incredible as it may sound, the poor child was actually dying of grief and what made the case even more pathetic was the fact that, all unknown to him, his brother stood at his side all the time, fully conscious of his misery and himself half-distracted at the failure of his repeated attempts to touch him or speak to him.

Affairs were still in this most pitiable condition on the third evening after the accident, when Cyril's attention was drawn to the two brothers, he cannot tell how. "He just happened to be passing," he says; yet surely the will of the Lords of Compassion guided him to the scene. Poor Walter lay exhausted yet sleepless

alone in his desolation, so far as he knew, though all the time his sorrowing brother stood beside him. Lancelot, free from the chains of the flesh, could see and hear Cyril, so obviously the first thing to do was to soothe his pain with a promise of friendship and help in communicating with his brother.

As soon as the dead boy's mind was thus cheered with hope, Cyril turned to the living one, and tried with all his strength to impress upon his brain the knowledge that his brother stood beside him, not dead, but living and loving as of yore. But all his efforts were in vain; the dull apathy of grief so filled poor Walter's mind that no suggestion from without could enter, and Cyril knew not what to do. Yet so deeply was he moved by the sad sight, so intense was his sympathy and so firm his determination to help in some way or other at any cost of strength to himself, that somehow (even to this day he cannot tell how) he found himself able to touch and speak to the heart-broken child.

Putting aside Walter's questions as to who he was and how he came there, he went straight to the point, telling him that his brother stood beside him, trying hard to make him hear his constantly repeated assurances that he was not dead, but living and yearning to help and comfort him. Little Walter longed to believe, yet hardly dared to hope; but Cyril's eager insistence vanquished his doubts at last, and he said, "Oh! I do believe you, because you're so kind; but if I could only see him, then I should know, then I should be quite sure; and if I could only hear his voice telling me he was happy, I shouldn't mind a bit his going away again afterwards."

Young though he was at the work, Cyril knew enough to be aware that Walter's wish was one not ordinarily granted, and was beginning regretfully to tell him so, when suddenly he felt a Presence that all the helpers know, and though no word was spoken it was borne in upon his mind that instead of what he had meant to say, he was to promise Walter the boon his heart desired. "Wait till I come back," he said, "and you shall see him then." And then, he vanished.

That one touch from the Master had shown him what to do and how to do it, and he rushed to fetch the older friend who had so often helped him before. This older man had not yet retired for the night, but on hearing Cyril's hurried summons, he lost no time in accompanying him, and in a few minutes, they were back at Walter's bedside. The poor child was just beginning to believe it all a lovely dream, and his delight and relief when Cyril reappeared were beautiful to see. Yet how much more beautiful was the scene a moment later, when, in obedience to a word from the Master, the elder man materialized the eager Lancelot, and the living and the dead stood hand in hand once more!

Now in very truth for both the brothers had sorrow been turned into joy unspeakable, and again and again they both declared that now they should never feel sad anymore, because they knew that death had no power to part them. Nor was their gladness damped even when Cyril explained carefully to them, at his older friend's suggestion, that this strange physical reunion would not be repeated, but that all day long Lancelot would be near Walter, even though the latter could not see him, and every night Walter would slip out of his body and be consciously with his brother once more.

Hearing this, poor weary Walter sank to sleep at once and proved its truth and was amazed to find with what hitherto unknown rapidity he and his brother could fly together from one to another of their old familiar haunts. Cyril thoughtfully warned him that he would probably forget most of his freer life when he awoke next day; but by rare good fortune he did not forget, as so many of us do. Perhaps the shock of the great joy had somewhat aroused the latent psychic faculty which belongs to the Celtic blood; at any rate he forgot no single detail of all that had happened, and next morning he burst upon the house of mourning with a wondrous tale which suited it but ill.

His parents thought that grief had turned his brain, and, since he is now the heir, they have been watching long and anxiously for further symptoms of insanity, which happily they have not found. They still think him a monomaniac on this point, though they fully recognize that his "delusion" has saved his life; but his old nurse (who is a Catholic) is firm in her belief that all he says is true that the Lord Jesus, who was once a child himself, took pity on that other child as he lay dying of grief, and sent one of His angels to bring his brother back to him from the dead as a reward for a love which was stronger than death. Sometimes popular superstition gets a good deal nearer to the heart of things than does educated skepticism!

Nor does the story end here, for the good work begun that night is still progressing, and none can say how far the influence of that one act may ramify. Walter's astral consciousness, once having been thus thoroughly awakened, remains in activity; every morning he brings back into his physical brain the memory of his night's adventures with his brother; every night they meet their dear friend Cyril, from whom they have learned so much about the wonderful new world that has opened before them, and the other worlds to come that lie higher yet. Under Cyril's guidance they also the living and the dead alike have become eager and earnest members of the band of helpers; and probably for years to come until Lancelot's vigorous young astral body disintegrates many a dying child will have cause to be grateful to these three who are trying to pass on to others something of the joy that they have themselves received.

Nor is it to the dead alone that these new converts have been of use, for they have sought and found some other living children who show consciousness on the astral plane during sleep; and one at least of those whom they have thus brought to Cyril has already proved a valuable little recruit to the children's band, as well as a very kind little friend down here on the physical plane.

Those to whom all these ideas are new sometimes find it very difficult to understand how children can be of any use in the astral world. Seeing, they would say, that the astral body of a child must be undeveloped, and the ego thus limited by childhood on the astral as well as the physical plane, in what way could such an ego be of use, or be able to help towards the spiritual, mental, and moral evolution of humanity, which we are told is the chief concern of the helpers?

When first such a question was asked, shortly after the publication of one of these stories in our magazine, I sent it to Cyril himself, to see what he would say to it, and his answer was this:

"It is quite true, as the writer says, that I am only a boy, and know very little yet, and that I shall be much more useful when I have learnt more. But I am able to do a little even now because there are so many people who have learnt nothing about Theosophy yet, though they may know very much more than I do about everything else. And you see when you want to get to a certain place, a little boy

who knows the way can do more for you than a hundred wise men who don't know it?"

It may be added that when a child had been awakened upon the astral plane the development of the astral body would proceed so rapidly that he would very soon be in a position upon that plane but little inferior to that of the awakened adult, and would of course be much in advance, so far as usefulness is concerned, of the wisest man who was as yet un-awakened. But unless the ego expressing himself through the child-body possessed the necessary qualification of a determined yet loving disposition, and had clearly manifested it in his previous lives, no occultist would take the very serious responsibility of awakening him upon the astral plane. When, however their karma is such that it is possible for them to be thus aroused, children very often prove most efficient helpers, and throw themselves into their work with a whole-souled devotion which is very beautiful to see. And so is fulfilled once more the ancient prophecy "a little child shall lead them."

Another question that suggests itself to one's mind in reading this last story of the two brothers is this: Since Cyril was somehow able to materialize himself by sheer force of love and pity and strength of will, is it not strange that Lancelot, who had been trying so much longer to communicate, had not succeeded in doing the same thing.

Well, there is of course no difficulty in seeing why poor Lancelot was unable to communicate with his brother, for that inability is simply the normal condition of affairs, the wonder is that Cyril was able to materialize himself, *not* that Lancelot was not. Not only, however, was the feeling probably stronger in Cyril's case, but he also knew exactly what he wanted to do - knew that such a thing as materialization was a possibility and had some general idea as to how it was done while Lancelot naturally knew nothing of all this then, though he does now.

— — —

CHAPTER XI

Wrecks And Catastrophes

Sometimes it is possible for members of the band of helpers to avert impending catastrophes of a somewhat larger order. In more than one case when the captain of a vessel has been carried unsuspecting far out of his course by some unknown current or through some mistaken reckoning, and has thereby run into serious danger, it has been possible to prevent shipwreck by repeatedly impressing upon his mind a feeling that something was wrong; and although this generally comes through into the captain's brain merely as a vaguely warning intuition, yet if it occurs again and again he is almost certain to give it some attention and take such precautions as suggest themselves to him.

In one case, for example, in which the master of a barque was much nearer into the land than he supposed, he was again and again pressed to heave the lead, and though he resisted this suggestion for some time as being unnecessary and absurd, he at last gave the order in a somewhat hesitating way. The result astounded him, and he at once put his vessel about and stood off from the coast, though it was not until morning came that he realized how very close he had been to an appalling disaster.

Often, however, a catastrophe is karmic in its nature, and consequently cannot be averted; but it must not therefore be supposed that in such cases no help can be given. It may be that the people concerned are destined to die, and therefore cannot be saved from death; but in many cases they may still be to some extent prepared for it and may certainly be helped upon the other side after it is over. Indeed, it may be definitely stated that wherever a great catastrophe of any kind takes place, there is also a special sending of help.

Two the recent cases in which such help off was given the were sinking of the *Drummond Castle* Cape Ushant and terrible the cyclone which devastated the city of St Louis in America. On both these occasions a few minutes' notice was given, and the helpers did their best to calm and raise men's minds, so that when the shock came upon them it would be less disturbing than it might otherwise have been. Naturally, however, the greater part of the work done with the victims in both these calamities was done upon the astral plane after they had left their physical bodies but of this we shall speak later.

It is sad to relate how often when some catastrophe is impending the helpers are hindered in their kindly offices by wild panic among those whom the danger threatens - or sometimes, worse still, by a mad outburst of drunkenness among those whom they are trying to assist. Many a ship has gone to her doom with almost every soul on board mad with drink, and therefore utterly incapable of profiting by any assistance offered either before death or for a very long time afterwards.

If it should ever happen to any of us to find ourselves in a position of imminent danger which we can do nothing to avert, we should try to remember that help is certainly near us, and that it rests entirely with ourselves to make the helper's work easy or difficult. If we face the danger calmly and bravely, recognizing that the true ego can in no way be affected by it, our minds will then be open to receive the guidance which the helpers are trying to give, and this cannot but be best for us, whether its object be to save us from death or, when that is impossible, to conduct us safely through it.

Assistance of this latter kind has not infrequently been given in cases of accidents to individuals, as well as of more general catastrophes. It will be sufficient to mention one example as an illustration of what is meant. In one of the great storms which did so much damage around our coasts a few years ago, it happened that a fishing boat was capsized far out at sea. The only people on board were an old fisherman and a boy, and the former contrived to cling for a few minutes to the overturned boat. There was no physical help at hand, and even if there had been in such a raging storm it would have been impossible for anything to be done, so that the fisherman knew well enough that there was no hope of escape, and that death could only be a question of a few moments. He felt a great terror at the prospect, being especially impressed by the awful loneliness of that vast waste of waters, and he was also much troubled with thoughts of his wife and family, and the difficulties in which they would be left by his sudden decease.

A passing helper seeing all this endeavoured to comfort him but finding his mind too much disturbed to be impressionable, she thought it advisable to show herself to him in order to assist him the better. In relating the story afterwards she said that the change which came over the fisherman's face at sight of her was wonderful and beautiful to see; with the shining form standing upon the boat above him he could not think that an angel had been sent to comfort him in his trouble, and therefore he felt that not only would he himself be carried safely through the gates of death, but his family would assuredly be looked after also. So, when death came to him a few moments later, he was in a frame of mind very different from the terror and perplexity which had previously overcome him; and naturally when he recovered consciousness upon the astral plane and found the "angel" still beside him he felt himself at home with her and was prepared to accept her advice as regards the new life upon which he had entered.

Sometime later the same helper was engaged in another piece of work of very similar character, the story of which she has since told as fellows: "You remember that steamer that went down in the cyclone at the end of last November; I betook myself to the cabin where about a dozen women had been shut in, and found them wailing in the most pitiful manner, sobbing, and moaning with fear. The ship had to founder - no aid was possible and to go out of the world in this state of frantic terror is the worst possible way to enter the next. So, in order to calm them I materialized myself, and of course they thought I was an angel, poor souls; they all fell on their knees and prayed me to save them, and one poor mother pushed her baby into my arms imploring me to save that at least. They soon grew quiet and composed as we talked, and the wee baby went to sleep smiling, and presently they all fell asleep peacefully, and I filled their minds with thoughts of the heaven-world, so that they did not wake up when the ship made her final plunge downwards. I went down with them to ensure their sleeping through the last moments, and they never stirred as their sleep became death."

Evidently in this case, too, those who were thus helped had not only the enormous advantage of being enabled to meet death calmly and reasonably, but also the still greater one of being received on its farther shore by one whom they were already disposed to love and trust one who thoroughly understood the new world in which they found themselves, and could not only reassure them as to their safety, but advise them how to order their lives under these much altered circumstances. And this brings us to the consideration of one of the largest and most important departments of the work of invisible helpers, the guidance and assistance which they are able to give to the dead.

— — —

CHAPTER XII

Work Among The Dead

It is one of the many evils resulting from the absurdly erroneous teaching as to conditions after death, which is unfortunately current in our western world, that those who have recently shaken off this mortal coil are usually much puzzled and often very seriously frightened at finding everything so different from what their religion had led them to expect. The mental attitude of a large number of such people was pithily voiced the other day by an English general, who three days after his death met one of the band of helpers whom he had known in physical life. After expressing his great relief that he had at last found someone with whom he was able to communicate, his first remark was: "But if I am dead, where am I? For if this is heaven, I don't think much of it; and if it is hell, it is better than I expected."

But unfortunately, a far greater number take things less philosophically. They have been taught that all men are destined to eternal flames except a favoured few who are superhumanly good; and since a very small amount of self-examination convinces them that they do not belong to *that* category, they are but too often in a condition of panic terror, dreading every moment that the new world in which they find themselves may dissolve and drop them into the clutches of the devil, in whom they have been sedulously taught to believe. In many cases they spend long periods of acute mental suffering before they can free themselves from the fatal influence of this blasphemous doctrine of everlasting punishment - before they can realize that the world is governed, not according to the caprice of a hideous demon who gloats over human anguish, but according to a benevolent and wonderfully patient law of evolution, which is absolutely just indeed, but yet again and again offers to man opportunities of progress, if he will but take them, at every stage of his career.

It ought in fairness to be mentioned that it is only among what are called protestant communities that this terrible evil assumes its most aggravated form. The great Roman Catholic Church, with its doctrine of purgatory, approaches much more nearly to a conception of the astral plane, and it devout members at any rate realize that the state in which they find themselves shortly after death is merely a temporary one, and that it is their business to endeavour to raise themselves out of it as soon as may be by intense spiritual aspiration, while they accept any suffering which may come to them as necessary for the wearing away of the imperfections in their character before they can pass to higher and brighter regions.

It will thus be seen that there is plenty of work for the helpers to do among the newly dead, for in the vast majority of cases they need to be calmed and reassured, to be comforted and instructed. In the astral, just as in the physical world, there are many who are but little disposed to take advice from those who know better than they; yet the very strangeness of the conditions surrounding them renders many of the dead willing to accept the guidance of those to whom these conditions are obviously familiar; and many a man's stay on that plane has been considerably shortened by the earnest efforts of this band of energetic workers.

Not, be it understood, that the karma of the dead man can in any way be interfered with; he has built for himself during life an astral body of a certain degree of density, and until that body is sufficiently dissolved, he cannot pass on into the heaven-world beyond; but he need not lengthen the period necessary for that process by adopting an improper attitude.

All students ought clearly to grasp the truth that the length of a man's astral life after he has put off his physical body depends mainly upon two factors, the nature of his past physical life, and his attitude of mind after what we call death. During his earth life he is constantly influencing the building of matter into his astral body. He affects it directly by the passions, emotions, and desires which he allows to hold sway over him; he affects it indirectly by the action upon it of his thoughts from above, and of the details of his physical life, his continence or his debauchery, his cleanliness or his uncleanliness, his food and his drink from below.

If by persistence in perversity along any of these lines he is so stupid as to build for himself a coarse and gross astral vehicle, habituated to responding only to the lower vibrations of the plane, he will find himself after death bound to that plane during and long and slow process of that body's disintegration. On the other hand, if by decent and careful living he gives himself a vehicle mainly composed of finer material, he will have very much less *post-mortem* trouble and discomfort, and his evolution will proceed much more rapidly and easily.

This much is generally understood, but the second great factor, his attitude of mind after death seems often to be forgotten. The desirable thing is for him to realize his position on this particular little arc of his evolution to learn that he is at this stage withdrawing steadily inward towards the plane of the true ego, and that consequently it is his business to disengage his thoughts as far as may be from things physical, and to fix his attention more and more upon those spiritual matters which will occupy him during his life in the heaven-world. By doing this he will greatly facilitate the natural astral disintegration and will avoid the sadly common mistake of unnecessarily delaying himself upon the lower levels of what should be so temporary a residence.

But many of the dead very considerably retard the process of dissolution by clinging passionately to the earth which they have left;

they simply will not turn their thoughts and desires upward but spend their time in struggling with all their might to keep in full touch with the physical plane, thus causing great trouble to anyone who may be trying to help them. Earthly matters are the only ones in which they have had any living interest, and they cling to them with desperate tenacity even after death. Naturally as time passes on, they find it increasingly difficult to keep hold of things down here, but instead of welcoming and encouraging this process of gradual refinement and spiritualization they resist it vigorously by every means in their power.

Of course, the mighty force of evolution is eventually too strong for them, and they are swept on in its beneficent current, yet they fight every step of the way, thereby not only causing themselves a vast amount of entirely unnecessary pain and sorrow, but also very seriously delaying their upward progress and prolonging their stay in astral regions to an almost indefinite extent. In convincing them that this ignorant and disastrous opposition to the cosmic will is contrary to the laws of nature and persuading them to adopt an attitude of mind which is the exact reversal of it, lies a great part of the work of those who are trying to help.

It happens occasionally that the dead are earthbound by anxiety, anxiety sometimes about duties unperformed or debts undischarged, but more often on account of wife or children left unprovided for. In such cases as this it has more than once been necessary, before the dead man was satisfied to pursue his upward path in peace, that the helper should to some extent act as his representative upon the physical plane and attend on his behalf to the settlement of the business which was troubling him. An illustration taken from our recent experience will perhaps make this clearer.

One of the band of pupils was trying to assist a poor man who had died in one of our western cities but found it impossible to withdraw his mind from earthly things because of his anxiety about two young children whom his death had left without means of support. He had been a working man of some sort, and had been unable to lay by any money for them; his wife had died some two years previously and his landlady, though exceedingly kindhearted and very willing to do anything in her power for them, was herself far too poor to be able to adopt them, and very reluctantly came to the conclusion that she would be obliged to hand them over to the parish authorities. This was a great grief to the dead father, though he could not blame the landlady, and was himself unable to suggest any other course.

Our friend asked him whether he had no relative to whom he could entrust them, but the father knew of none. He had a younger brother, he said, who would certainly have done something for him in this extremity, but he had lost sight of him for fifteen years and did not even know whether he was living or dead. When last heard of he had been apprenticed to a carpenter in the north, and he was then described as a steady young fellow who, if he lived, would surely get on.

The clues at hand were certainly very slight, but since there seemed no other prospect of help for the children, our friend thought it worthwhile to make a special effort to follow them up. Taking the dead man with him he commenced a patient search after the brother in the town indicated; and after a great deal of trouble, they were actually successful in finding him. He was now a master carpenter in a fairly flourishing way of business married, but without children though earnestly desiring them, and therefore apparently just the man for the emergency.

The question now was how the information could be conveyed to this brother. Fortunately, he was found to be so far impressionable that the circumstances of his brother's death and the destitution of his children could be put vividly before him in a dream, and this was repeated three times, the place and even the name of the landlady being clearly indicated to him. He was immensely impressed by this recurring vision, and discussed it earnestly with his wife, who advised him to write to the address given. This he did not like to do but was strongly inclined to travel down into the west country, find out whether there was such a house as that which he had seen and if so, make some excuse to call there. He was a busy man, however, and he finally decided that he could not afford to lose a day's work for what after all might well prove to be nothing but the baseless fabric of a dream.

The attempt along these lines having apparently failed, it was determined to try another method, so one of the helpers wrote a letter to the man detailing the circumstances of his brother's death and the position of the children, exactly as he had seen them in his dream. On receipt of this confirmation, he no longer hesitated but set off the very next day for the town indicated and was received with open arms by the kind-hearted landlady. It had been easy enough for the helpers to persuade her, good soul that she was, to keep the children with her for a few days on the chance that something or other would turn up for them, and she has ever since congratulated herself that she did so. The carpenter of course took the children back with him and provided them with a happy home, and the dead father, now no longer anxious, passed rejoicing on his upward journey.

Since some Theosophical writers have felt it their duty to insist in vigorous terms upon the evils so frequently attendant upon the holding of spiritual séances, it is only fair to admit that on several occasions good work similar to that of the helper in the case just described has been done through the agency of a medium or of someone present at a circle. Thus, though spiritualism has too often detained souls who but for it would have attained speedier liberation, it must be set to the credit of its account that it has also furnished the means of escape to others, and thus opened up the path of advancement for them. There have been instances in which the defunct has been able to appear unassisted to his relatives or friends and explain his wishes to them; but these are naturally rare, and most souls who are earth-bound by anxieties of the kind indicated can satisfy themselves only by means of the services of the medium or the conscious helper.

Another case very frequently encountered on the astral plane is that of the man who cannot believe that he is dead at all. Indeed, most people consider the very fact that they are still conscious to be an absolute proof that they have not passed through the portals of death; somewhat of a satire this, if one thinks of it, on the practical value of our much-vaunted belief in the immortality of the soul! However, they may have labeled themselves during life, the great majority of those who die, in this country at any rate, show themselves by their subsequent attitude to have been to all intents and purposes materialists at heart; and those who on earth have honestly called themselves so are often no more difficult to deal with than others who would have been shocked at the very name.

A very recent instance was that of a scientific man who, finding himself fully conscious, and yet under conditions differing radically from any that he had ever experienced before, had persuaded himself that he was still alive, and merely the victim of a prolonged and unpleasant dream. Fortunately for him there happened to be among the band of those able to function upon the astral plane a son of an old friend of his, a young man whose father had commissioned him to search for the departed scientist and endeavour to render him some assistance. When after some trouble the youth found and accosted him, he frankly admitted that he was in a condition of great bewilderment and discomfort, but still clung desperately to his dream hypothesis as on the whole the most probable explanation of what he saw, and even went so far as to suggest that his visitor was nothing but a dream-figure himself!

At last, however, he so far gave way as to propose a kind of test, and said to the young man, "If you are, as you assert, a living person, and the son of my old friend, bring me from him some message that shall prove to me your objective reality." Now although under all ordinary conditions of the physical plane the giving of any kind of phenomenal proof is strictly forbidden to the pupils of the Masters, it seemed as though a case of this kind hardly came under the rules and therefore, when it had been ascertained that there was no objection on the part of higher authorities, an application was made to the father, who at once sent a message referring to a series of events which had occurred before the son's birth. This convinced the dead man of the real existence of his young friend, and therefore of the plane upon which they were both functioning; and as soon as he felt this established, his scientific training at once reasserted itself, and he became exceeding eager to acquire all possible information about this new region.

Of course, the message which he so readily accepted as evidence was in reality no proof at all since the facts to which it referred might have been read from his own mind or from the records of the past by any creature possessed of astral senses! But his ignorance of these possibilities enabled this definite impression to be made upon him, and the Theosophical instruction which his young friend is now nightly giving to him will undoubtedly have a stupendous effect upon his future, for it cannot but greatly modify not only the heaven-state which lies immediately before him but also his next incarnation upon earth.

The main work, then, done for the newly dead by our helpers is that of soothing and comforting them of delivering them, when possible, from the terrible though unreasoning fear which but too often seizes them, and not only causes them much unnecessary suffering, but retards their progress to higher spheres and of enabling them as far as may be to comprehend the future that lies before them.

Others who have been longer on the astral plane may also receive much help, if they will but accept it, from explanations and advice as to their course through its different stages. They may, for example, be warned of the danger and delay caused by attempting to communicate with the living through a medium, and sometimes (though rarely) an entity already drawn into a spiritualistic circle may be guided into higher and healthier life. Teaching thus given to persons on this plane is by no means lost for though the memory of it cannot of course be directly carried over to the next incarnation, there always remains the real inner knowledge, and therefore the strong predisposition to accept it immediately when heard again in the new life.

A rather remarkable instance of service rendered to the dead was the first achievement of a very recent recruit to the band of helpers one who is hardly as yet a fully-fledged member. This young aspirant had not long before lost an aged relation for whom he had felt an especially warm affection; and his earliest request was to be taken by a more experienced friend to visit her in the hope that he might be of some service to her. This was done and the effect of the meeting of the living and the dead was very beautiful and touching. The older person's astral life was already approaching its end, but a condition of apathy, dullness and uncertainty prevented her from making any immediate progress.

But when the boy, who had been so much to her in earth-life, stood once more before her and dissolved by the sunlight of his love the grey mist of depression which had gathered around her, she was aroused from her stupor; and soon she understood that he had come in order to explain to her situation, and to tell her of the glories of the higher life toward which her thoughts and aspirations ought now to be directed. But when this was fully realized, there was such an awakening of dormant feeling in her and such an outrush of devoted affection towards her earnest young helper, that the last fetters which bound her to the astral life were broken, and that one great outburst of love and gratitude swept her forthwith into the higher consciousness of the heaven-world. Truly there is no greater and more beneficent power in the universe than that of pure, unselfish love.

— — —

CHAPTER XIII

Other Branches Of The Work

But turning back again now from the all-important work among the dead to the consideration of the work among the living, we must briefly indicate a great branch of it, without a notice of which our account of the labours of our invisible helpers would indeed be incomplete, and that is the immense amount which is done by suggestion - by simply putting good thoughts into the minds of those who are ready to receive them.

Let there be no mistake as to what is meant here. It would be perfectly easy, easy to a degree which would be quite incredible to those who do not understand the subject practically for a helper to dominate the mind of any average man, and make him think just as he pleased, and that without arousing the faintest suspicion of any outside influence in the mind of the subject. But however admirable the result might be, such a proceeding would be entirely inadmissible. All that may be done is to throw the good thought into the person's mind as one among the hundreds that are constantly sweeping through it; whether the man takes it up, makes it his own, and acts upon it, depends upon himself entirely. Were it otherwise, it is obvious that all the good karma of the action would accrue to the helper only, for the subject would have been a mere tool, and not an actor which is not what is desired?

The assistance given in this way is exceedingly varied in character. The consolation of those who are suffering or in sorrow at once suggests itself, as does also the endeavour to guide toward the truth those who are earnestly seeking it. When a person is spending much anxious thought upon some spiritual or metaphysical problem, it is often possible to put the solution into his mind without his being at all aware that it comes from external agency.

A pupil too may often be employed as an agent in what can hardly be described otherwise than as the answering of prayer; for though it is true that any earnest spiritual desire, such as might be supposed to find its expression in prayer, is itself a force which automatically brings about certain results, it is also a fact that such a spiritual effort offers an opportunity of influence to the Powers of Good, of which they are not slow to take advantage; and it is sometimes the privilege of a willing helper to be made the channel through which their energy is poured forth. What is said of prayers is true to an even greater extent of meditation, for those to whom this higher exercise is a possibility.

Besides these more general methods of help there are also special lines open only to the few. Again, and again such pupils as are fitted for the work have been employed to suggest true and beautiful thoughts to authors, poets, artists, and musicians; but obviously it is not every helper who is capable of being used in this way.

Sometimes, though more rarely, it is possible to warn persons of the danger to their moral development of some course which they are pursuing, to clear away evil influences from about some person or place, or to counteract the machinations of black magicians. It is not often that direct instruction in the great truths of nature can be given to people outside the circle of occult students, but occasionally it is possible to do something in that way by putting before the minds of preachers and teachers a wider range of thought or a more liberal view of some question than they would otherwise have taken.

Naturally as an occult student progress on the Path he attains a wider sphere of usefulness. Instead of assisting individuals only, he learns how classes, nations and races are dealt with, and he is entrusted with a gradually increasing share of the higher and more important work done by the adepts themselves. As he acquires the requisite power and knowledge, he begins to wield the greater forces of the mental and the astral planes and is shown how to make the utmost possible use of each favourable cyclic influence. He is brought into relation with those great Nirmanakayas who are sometimes symbolized as the Stones of the Guardian Wall, and he becomes at first of course in the very humblest capacity

one of the and, of their almoners and learns how those forces are dispersed which are the fruit of their sublime self-sacrifice. Thus, he rises gradually higher and higher until, blossoming at length into adept ship, he is able to take his full share of the responsibility which lies upon the Masters of Wisdom, and to help others along the road which he has trodden.

On the mental plane the work differs somewhat, since teaching can be both given and received in a much more direct, rapid, and perfect manner, while the influences set in motion are infinitely more powerful, because acting on so much higher a level. But (though it is useless to speak of it in detail at present, since so few of us are yet able to function consciously upon this plane during life) here also and even higher still there is always plenty of work to be done, as soon as ever we can make ourselves capable of doing it; and there is certainly no fear that for countless aeons we shall ever find ourselves without a career of unselfish usefulness open before us.

— — —

CHAPTER XIV

The Qualifications Required

How, it may be asked, are we to make ourselves capable of sharing in this great work? Well, there is no mystery as to the qualifications which are needed by one who aspires to be a helper; the difficulty is not in learning what they are, but in developing them in oneself. To some extent they have been already incidentally described, but it is nevertheless as well that they should be set out fully and categorically.

Single-mindedness. The first requisite is that we shall have recognized the great work which the master's would have us do, and that it shall be for us the one great interest in our lives. We must learn to distinguish not only between useful and useless work, but between the different kinds of useful work, so that we may each devote ourselves to the very highest of which we are capable, and not fritter away our time in labouring at something which, however good it may be for the man who cannot yet do anything better, is unworthy of the knowledge and capacity which should be ours as Theosophists. A man who wishes to be considered eligible for employment on higher planes must begin by doing the utmost that lies in his power in the way of definite work for Theosophy down here.

Of course, I do not for a moment mean that we are to neglect the ordinary duties of life. We should certainly do well to undertake no new worldly duties of any sort, but those which we have already bound upon our shoulders have become a karmic obligation which we have no right to neglect. Unless we have done to the full the duties which karma has laid upon us, we are not free for the higher work. But this higher work must nevertheless be to us the one thing really worth living for the constant background of a life which is consecrated to the service of the Masters of Compassion.

Perfect self-control. Before we can be safely trusted with the wider powers of the astral life, we must have ourselves perfectly in hand. Our temper, for example, must be thoroughly under control, so that nothing that we may see or hear can cause real irritation in us, for the consequences of such irritation would be far more serious on that plane than on this. The force of thought is always an enormous power, but down here it is reduced and deadened by the heavy physical brain-particles which it has to set in motion. In the astral world it is far freer and more potent, and for a man with fully awakened faculty to feel anger against a person there would be to do him serious and perhaps even fatal injury.

Not only do we need control of temper, but control of nerve, so that none of the fantastic or terrible sights that we may encounter may be able to shake our dauntless courage. It must be remembered that the pupil who awakens a man upon the astral plane incurs thereby a certain amount of responsibility for his actions and for his safety, so that unless his neophyte had courage to stand alone the whole of the older worker's time would be wasted in hovering round to protect him, which it would be manifestly unreasonable to expect.

It is to make sure of this control of nerve, and to fit them for the work that has to be done, that candidates are always made, now as in days of old, to pass what are called the tests of earth, water, air, and fire.

In other words, they have to learn with that absolute certainty that comes not by theory, but by practical experience, that in their astral bodies none of these elements can by any possibility be hurtful to them - that none can oppose any obstacle in the way the work which they have to do.

In this physical body we are fully convinced that fire will burn us, that water will drown us, that the solid rock forms an impassable barrier to our progress, that we cannot with safety launch ourselves unsupported into the ambient air. So deeply is this conviction ingrained in us that it costs most men a good deal of effort to overcome the instinctive action which follows from it, and to realize that in the astral body the densest rock offers no impediment to their freedom of motion, that they may leap with impunity from the highest cliff, and plunge with the most absolute confidence into the heart of the raging volcano or the deepest abysses of the fathomless ocean.

Yet until a man *knows* this - knows it sufficiently to act upon his knowledge instinctively and confidently, he is comparatively useless for astral work, since in emergencies that are constantly arising, he would be perpetually paralyzed by imaginary disabilities. So, he has to go through his tests, and through many another strange experience to meet face to face with calm courage the most terrifying apparitions amid the most loathsome surroundings to show in fact that his nerve may be thoroughly trusted under any and all of the varied groups of circumstances in which he may at any moment find himself.

Further, we need control of mind and of desire; of mind, because without the power of concentration it would be impossible to do good work amid all the distracting currents of the astral plane; of desire, because in that strange world to desire is very often to have, and unless this part of our nature were well controlled we might perchance find ourselves face to face with creations of our own of which we should be heartily ashamed.

Calmness. This is another most important point, the absence of all worry and depression. Much of the work consists in soothing those who are disturbed, and cheering those who are in sorrow; and how can a helper do that work if his own aura is vibrating with constant fuss and worry, or grey with the deadly gloom that comes from perpetual depression? Nothing is more hopelessly fatal to occult progress or usefulness than our nineteenth century habit of ceaselessly worrying over trifles of eternally making mountains out of molehills. Many of us simply spend our lives in magnifying the most absurd trivialities in solemnly and elaborately going to work to make ourselves miserable about nothing.

Surely we who are Theosophists ought, at any rate, to have got beyond this stage of irrational worry and causeless depression; surely we, who are trying to acquire some definite knowledge of the cosmic order, ought by this time to have realized that the optimistic view of everything is always nearest to the divine view, and therefore to the truth, because only that in any person which is good and beautiful can by any possibility be permanent, while the evil must by its very nature be temporary. In fact, as Browning said, "the evil is null, is naught, is silence implying sound," while above and beyond it all "the soul of things is sweet, the Heart of Being is celestial rest." So, they who know maintain unruffled calm, and with Their perfect sympathy combine the joyous serenity which comes from the certainty that all will at last be well; and those who wish to help must learn to follow Their example?

Knowledge. To be of use the man must at least have some knowledge of the nature of the plane on which he has to work, and the more knowledge he has in any and every direction the more useful he will be. He must fit himself for this task by carefully studying Theosophical literature; for he cannot expect those whose time is already so fully occupied to waste some of it in explaining to him what he might have learnt down here by taking the trouble to read the books. No one who is not already as earnest a student as his capacities and opportunities permit, need begin to think of himself as a candidate for astral work.

Unselfishness. It would seem scarcely needful to assist upon this as a qualification, for surely everyone who has made the least study of Theosophy must know that while the slightest taint of selfishness remains in a man, he is not yet fit to be entrusted with higher powers, not yet fit to enter upon a work of whose very essence it is that the worker should forget himself but to remember the good of others. He who is still capable of selfish thought, whose personality is still so strong in him that he can allow himself to be turned aside from his work by feelings of petty pride or suggestions of wounded dignity that man is not yet ready to show the selfless devotion of the helper.

Love. This, the last and greatest of the qualifications, is also the most misunderstood. Most emphatically it is not the cheap, namby-pamby backboneless sentimentalism which is always overflowing into vague platitudes and gushing generalities yet fears to stand firm for the right lest it should be branded by the ignorant as "unbrotherly." What is wanted is the love which is strong enough not to boast itself, but to act without talking about it - the intense desire for service which is ever on the watch for an opportunity to render it, even though it prefers to do so anonymously - the feeling which springs up in the heart of him who has realized the great work of the Logos, and having once seen it, knows that for him there can be in the three worlds no other course but to identify himself with it to the utmost limit of his power to become, in however humble a way, and at however great a distance, a tiny channel of that wondrous love of God which, like the peace of God, passed man's understanding.

These are the qualities toward the possession of which the helper must ceaselessly strive, and of which some considerable measure at least must be his before he can hope that the Great Ones who stand behind will deem him fit for full awakening. The ideal is in truth a high one, yet none need therefore turn away disheartened, nor think that while he is still but struggling toward it, he must necessarily remain entirely useless on the astral plane, for short of the responsibilities and dangers of that full awakening there is much that may safely and usefully be done.

There is hardly one among us who would not be capable of performing at least one definite act of mercy and good will each night while we are away from our bodies. Our condition when asleep is usually one of absorption in thought, be it remembered, a carrying on of the thoughts that have principally occupied us during the day, and especially of the last thought in the mind when sinking into sleep. Now if we make that last thought a strong intention to go and give help to someone whom we know to be in need of it, the soul when freed from the body will undoubtedly carry out that intention, and the help will be given. There are several cases on record in which, when this attempt has been made, the person thought of has been fully conscious of the effort of the would-be helper and has even seen his astral body in the act of carrying out the instructions impressed upon it.

Indeed, no one need sadden himself with the thought that he can have no part nor lot in this glorious work. Such a feeling would be entirely untrue, for everyone who can think can help. Nor need such useful action be confined to our hours of sleep. If you know (and who does not?) of someone who is in sorrow or suffering, though you may not be able consciously to stand in astral form by their bedside, you can nevertheless send them loving thoughts and earnest good wishes; and be well assured that such thoughts and wishes are real and living and strong that when you so send them they do actually go and work your will in proportion to the strength which you have put into them. Thoughts are things, intensely real things, visible enough to those whose eyes have been opened to see, and by their means the poorest man may bear his part in the good work of the world as fully as the richest. In this way at least, whether we can yet function consciously upon the astral plane or not, we all can join, and we all ought to join, the army of invisible helpers.

But the aspirant, who definitely desires to become one of the bands of astral helpers who are working under the direction of the great Masters of Wisdom, will make his preparation part of a far wider scheme of development. Instead of merely endeavouring to fit himself for this particular branch of their service, he will undertake with high resolution the far greater task of training himself to follow in their footsteps, of bending all the energies of his soul to attain even as they have attained, so that his power of helping the world may not be confined to the astral plane but may extend to those higher levels which are the true home of the divine self of man.

For him the path has been marked out long ago by the wisdom of those who have trodden it in days of old - a path of self-development which sooner or later all must follow, whether they choose to adopt it of their own free will, or to wait until, after many lives and an infinity of suffering, the slow, resistless force of evolution drives them along it among the laggards of the human family. But the wise man is he who eagerly enters upon it immediately, setting his face resolutely toward the goal of adept ship, in order that, being safe for ever from all doubt and fear and sorrow himself, he may help others into safety and happiness also. What are the steps of this Path of Holiness, as the Buddhists call it, and in what order they are arranged, let us see in our next chapter.

— — —

CHAPTER XV

The Probationary Path

Eastern books tell us that there are four means by which a man may be brought to the beginning of the path of spiritual advancement: 1. By the companionship of those who have already entered upon it. 2. By the hearing or reading of definite teaching on occult philosophy. 3. By enlightened reflection; that is to say, that by sheer force of hard thinking and close reasoning he may arrive at the truth, or some portion of it, for himself. 4. By the practice of virtue, which means that a long series of virtuous lives, though it does not necessarily involve any increase of intellectuality, does eventually develop in man sufficient intuition to enable him to grasp the necessity of entering upon the path, and show him in what direction it lies.

When, by one or another of these means, he has arrived at this point, the way to the highest adept-ship lies straight before him if he chooses to take it. In writing for students of occultism it is hardly necessary to say that at our present stage of development we cannot expect to learn all, or nearly all, about any but the lowest steps of this path; whilst of the highest we know little but the names, though we may got occasional glimpses of the indescribable glory which surrounds them.

According to the esoteric teachings these steps are grouped in three great divisions:

The probationary period, before any definite pledges are taken, or initiations (in the full sense of the word) are given. This carries a man to the level necessary to pass successfully through what in Theosophical books is usually called the critical period of the fifth round.

The period of pledged discipleship, or the path proper, whose four stages are often spoken of in Oriental books as the four paths of holiness. At the end of this the pupil obtains adept ship, the level which humanity should reach at the close of the seventh round.

What we may venture to call the official period, in which the adept takes a definite part (under the great Cosmic Law) in the government of the world, and holds a special office connected therewith, Of course every adept, every pupil even, when once definitely accepted, as we have seen in the earlier chapters takes a part in the great work of helping forward the evolution of man; but those standing on the higher levels take charge of special departments, and correspond in the cosmic scheme to the ministers of the crown in a well-ordered earthly state. It is not proposed to make any attempt in this book to treat of this official period; no information about it has ever been made public, and the whole subject is too far above our comprehension to be profitably dealt with in print. We will confine ourselves therefore to the two earlier divisions.

Before going into details of the probationary period it is well to mention that in most of the Eastern sacred books this stage is regarded as merely preliminary, and scarcely as part of the path at all, for they consider that the latter is really entered upon only when definite pledges have been given. Considerable confusion has been created by the fact that the numbering of the stages occasionally commences at this point, though more often at the beginning of the second great division; sometimes the stages themselves are counted, and sometimes the initiations leading into or out of them, so that in studying the books one has to be perpetually on one's guard to avoid misunderstanding.

This probationary period, however, differs considerably in character from the others; the divisions between its stages are less decidedly marked than are those of the higher groups, and the requirements are not so definite or so exacting. But it will be easier to explain this last point after giving a list of the five stages of this period, with their respective qualifications. The first four were very ably described by Mr. Mohini Mohun Chatterji in the first Transaction of the London Lodge, to which readers may be referred for fuller definitions of them than can be given here. Much exceedingly valuable information about them is also given by Mrs. Besant in her books *The Path of Discipleship and In the Outer Court.*

The names given to the stages will differ somewhat, for in those books the Hindu Sanskrit terminology was employed, whereas the Pali nomenclature used here is that of the Buddhist system; but although the subject is thus approached from a different side as it were, the qualifications exacted will be found to be precisely the same in effect even when the outward form varies. In the case of each word the mere dictionary meaning will first be given in parentheses and the explanation of it which is usually given by the teacher will follow. The first stage, then is called among Buddhists.

Manodvaravajjana (the opening of the doors of the mind, or perhaps escaping by the door of the mind) and in it the candidate acquires a firm intellectual conviction of the impermanence and worthlessness of mere earthly aims. This is often described as learning the difference between the real and the unreal; and to learn it often takes a long time and many hard lessons. Yet it is obvious that it must be the first step toward anything like real progress, for no man can enter whole-heartedly upon the path until he has definitely decided to "set his affection upon things above, not on things on the earth," and that decision comes from the certainty that nothing on earth has any value as compared with the higher life. This step is called by the Hindus the acquirement of Viveka or discrimination, and Mr. Sinnett speaks of it as the giving allegiance to the higher self.

Parikamma (preparation for action), the stage in which the candidate learns to do the right merely because it is right, without considering his own gain or loss either in this world or the future, and acquires, as the Eastern books put it, perfect indifference to the enjoyment of the fruit of his own actions. This indifference is the natural result of the previous step; for when the neophyte has once grasped the unreal and impermanent character of all earthly rewards, he ceases to crave for them; when once the radiance of the real has shone upon the soul, nothing below that can any longer be an object of desire. This higher indifference is called by the Hindus Vairagya.

Upacharo (attention or conduct), the stage in which what are called "the six qualifications" (the Shatsampatti of the Hindus) must be acquired. These are called in Pali:

a. Samo (quietude) that purity and calmness of thought which comes from perfect control of the mind, a qualification exceedingly difficult of attainment, and yet most necessary, for unless the mind moves only in obedience to the guidance of the will it cannot be a perfect instrument for the master's work in the future. This qualification is a very comprehensive one and includes within itself both the self-control and the calmness which were described in chapter xiv. as necessary for astral work.

b. Damo (subjugation) a similar mastery over, and therefore purity in, one's actions and words, a quality which again follows necessarily from its predecessor.

c. Uparti (cessation) explained as cessation from bigotry or from belief in the necessity of any act or ceremony prescribed by a particular religion so leading the aspirant to independence of thought and to a wide and generous tolerance.

d. Titikkha (endurance or forbearance) by which is meant the readiness to bear with cheerfulness whatever one's karma may bring upon one, and to part with anything and everything worldly whenever it may be necessary. It also includes the idea of complete absence of resentment for wrong, the man knowing that those who do him wrong are but the instruments of his own karma.

e. Samadhana (intentness) one-pointedness involving the incapability of being turned aside from one's path by temptation. This corresponds very closely with the single mind-ness spoken of in the previous chapter.

f. Saddha (faith) confidence in one's Master and oneself: confidence, that is, that the Master is a competent teacher, and that, however diffident the pupil may feel as to his own powers, he has yet within him that divine spark which when fanned into a flame will one day enable him to achieve even as his Master has done.

Anuloma (direct order or succession, signifying that its attainment follows as a natural consequence from the other three) the stage in which is acquired that intense desire for liberation from earthly life, and for union with the highest, which is called by the Hindus Mumukshatva.

Gotrabhu (the condition of fitness for initiation); in this stage the candidate gathers up, as it were, his previous acquisitions, and strengthens them to the degree necessary for the next great step, which will set his feet upon the path proper as an accepted pupil. The attainment of this level is followed very rapidly by initiation into the next grade. In answer to the question, "Who is the Gotrabhu?" Buddha says, "The man who is in possession of those conditions upon which the commencement of sanctification immediately ensues, he is the Gotrabhu

The wisdom necessary for the reception of the path of holiness is called Gotrabhu-gnana.

Now that we have hastily glanced at the steps of the probationary period, we must emphasize the point to which reference was made at the commencement that the *perfect* attainment of these accomplishments and qualifications is not expected at this early stage. As Mr. Mohini says, "If all these are equally strong, adept-ship is attained in the same incarnation." But such a result is of course extremely rare. It is in the direction of these acquirements that the candidate must ceaselessly strive, but it would be an error to suppose that no one has been admitted to the next step without possessing all of them in the fullest possible degree. Nor do they necessarily follow one another in the same definite order as the later steps; in fact, in many cases a man would be developing the various qualifications all at the same time, rather side by side than in regular succession.

It is obvious that a man might easily be working along a great part of this path even though he was quite unaware of its very existence, and no doubt many a good Christian, many an earnest freethinker is already far on the road that will eventually lead him to initiation, though he may never have heard the word occultism in his life. I mention these two classes especially, because in every other religion occult development is recognized as a possibility and would certainly therefore be intentionally sought by those who felt yearnings for something more satisfactory than the exoteric faiths.

We must also note that the steps of this probationary period are not separated by initiations in the full sense of the word, though they will certainly be studded with tests and trials of all sorts and on all planes, and may be relieved by encouraging experiences, and by hints and help whenever these may safely be given. We are apt sometimes to use the word initiation somewhat loosely, as for example when it is applied to such tests as have just been mentioned; properly speaking it refers only to the solemn ceremony at which a pupil is formally admitted to a higher grade by an appointed official, who in the name of the One Initiator receives his plighted vow, and puts into his hands the new key of knowledge which he is to use on the level to which he has now attained. Such an initiation is taken at the entrance to the division which we shall next consider and also at each passage from any one of its steps to the next.

— — —

CHAPTER XVI

The Path Proper

It is in the four stages of this division of the path that the ten Samyojana, or fetters which bind man to the circle of rebirth and hold him back from Nirvana, must be cast off. And here comes the difference between this period of pledged discipleship and the previous probation. No partial success in getting rid of these fetters is sufficient now; before a candidate can pass on from one of the steps to the next he must be *entirely* free from certain of these clogs; and when they are enumerated it will be seen how far-reaching this requirement is and there will be little cause to wonder at the statement made in the sacred books that seven incarnations are sometimes required to pass through this division of the path.

Each of these four steps or stages is again divided into four: for each has (1) its Maggo, or way, during which the student is striving to cast off the fetters; (2) its Phala (result or fruit) when he finds the results of his action in so doing showing themselves more and more; (3) its Bhavagga or consummation, the period when, the result having culminated, he is able to fulfil satisfactorily the work belonging to the step on which he now firmly stands; and (4) its Gotrabhu, meaning, as before, the time when he arrives at a fit state to receive the next initiation. The first stage is:

Sotapatti or Sohan. The pupil who has attained this level is spoken of as the Sowani or Sotapanna, "he who has entered the stream, "because from this period, though he may linger, though he may succumb to more refined temptations and turn aside from his course for a time, he can no longer fall back altogether from spirituality and become a mere worldling. He has entered upon the stream of definite higher human evolution, upon which all humanity must enter by the middle of the next round, unless they are to be left behind as temporary failures by the great life-wave, to wait for further progress until the next chain of worlds.

The pupil who is able to take this initiation has therefore already outstripped the majority of humanity to the extent of an entire round of all our seven planets, and in doing so has definitely secured himself against the possibility of falling out of the stream in the fifth round. He is consequently sometimes spoken of as "the saved" or "the safe one." It is from a misunderstanding of this idea that there arises the curious theory of salvation promulgated by a certain section of the Christian community. The "aeonian salvation" of which some of its documents speak is not, as has been blasphemously supposed by the ignorant, from eternal torture, but simply from wasting the rest of this aeon or dispensation by falling out of its line of progress. This also is the meaning, naturally, of the celebrated clause in the Athanasian Creed, "Whosoever will be saved, before all things it is necessary that he hold the catholic faith" (*See the Christian Creed*, p.91). The fetters which he must cast off before he can pass into the next stage are:

Sakkayaditthi: the delusion of self.

Vichikichchha: doubt or uncertainty.

Silabbataparamasa: superstition.

The first of these is the "I am I" consciousness, which as connected with the *personality* is nothing but an illusion and must be got rid of at the very first step of the real upward path. But to cast off this fetter completely means even more than this, for it involves the realization of the fact that the individuality also is in very truth one with the All, that it can therefore never have any interests opposed to those of its brethren, and that it is most truly progressing when it most assists the progress of others.

For the very sign and seal of the attainment of the Sotapatti level is the first entrance of the pupil into the plane next above the mental that which we usually call the buddhic. It may be nay, it will be the merest touch of the lowest sub-plane of that stupendously exalted condition that the pupil can as yet experience, even with his master's help but even that touch is something that can never be forgotten something that opens a new world before him and entirely revolutionizes his feelings and conceptions. Then for the first time, by means of the extended consciousness of that plane, he truly realizes the underlying unity of all, not as an intellectual conception merely, but as a definite fact that is patent to his opened eyes; then first he really knows something of the world in which he lives then first he gets some slight glimpse of what the love and compassion of the great master's must be.

As to the second fetter, a word of caution is necessary. We who have been trained in European habits of thought are unhappily so familiar with the idea that a blind unreasoning adhesion to certain dogmas may be claimed from a disciple, that or hearing that occultism considers *doubt* as an obstacle to progress, we are likely to suppose that it also requires the same unquestioning faith from its followers as modern superstitions do. No idea could be more certainly false.

It is true that doubt (or rather uncertainty) on certain questions is a bar to spiritual progress, but the antidote to that doubt is not blind faith (which is itself considered as a fetter, as will presently be seen) but the certainty of conviction founded on individual experiment or mathematical reasoning. While a child doubted the accuracy of the multiplication table, he would hardly acquire proficiency in the higher mathematics; but his doubts could be satisfactorily cleared up only by his attaining a comprehension, founded on reasoning or experiment, that the statements contained in the table are true. He believes that twice two are four, not merely because he has been told so, but because it has become to him a self-evident fact. And this is exactly the method, and the only method, of resolving doubt known to occultism.

Vichikichchha has been defined as doubt of the doctrines of karma and reincarnation, and of the efficacy of the method of attaining the highest good by this path of holiness; and the casting off of this Samyojana is the arriving at absolute certainty, based either upon personal first-hand knowledge or upon reason, that the occult teaching upon these points is true.

The third fetter to be got rid of comprehends all kinds of unreasoning or mistaken belief, all dependence on the efficacy of outward rites and ceremonies to purify the heart. He who would cast it off must learn to depend upon himself alone, not upon others, nor upon the outer husk of any religion.

The first three fetters are in a coherent series. The difference between individuality and personality being fully realized, it is then possible to some extent to appreciate the actual course of reincarnation, and so as to dispel all doubt on that head. This done, the knowledge of the spiritual permanence of the true ego gives rise to reliance on one's own spiritual strength, and so dispels superstition.

II. Sakadagami. The pupil who has entered upon this second stage is spoken of as a Sakridagamin, "the man who returns but once" signifying that a man who has reached this level should need but one more incarnation before attaining arahatship. At this step no additional fetters are cast off, but the pupil is occupied in reducing to a minimum those which still enchain him. It is, however, usually a period of considerable psychic and intellectual advancement.

If what are commonly called psychic faculties have not been previously acquired, they must be developed at this stage, as without them it would be impossible to assimilate the knowledge which must now be given, or to do the higher work for humanity in which the pupil is now privileged to assist. He must have the astral consciousness at his command during his physical waking life, and during sleep the heaven-world will be open before him for the consciousness of a man when away from his physical body is always one stage higher than it is while he is still burdened with the house of flesh.

III. Anagami. The Anagamin (he who does not return) is so called because, having reached this stage, he ought to be able to attain the next one in the life he is then living. He enjoys, while moving through the round of his daily work, all the splendid possibilities of progress given by the full possession of the priceless faculties of the heaven-world, and when he leaves his physical vehicle at night he enters once more into the wonderfully widened consciousness that belongs to the buddhi. In this step he finally gets rid of any lingering remains of the two fetters of

Kamaraga attachment to the enjoyment of sensation, typified by earthly love, and

Patigha: all possibility of anger or hatred.

The student who has cast off these fetters can no longer be swayed by the influence of his senses either in the direction of love or hatred and is free from either attachment to or impatience of physical plane conditions.

Here again we must guard against a possible misconception one with which we frequently meet. The purest and noblest human love *never* dies away is *never* in any way diminished by occult training; on the contrary, it is increased and widened until it embraces all with the same fervour which at first was lavished on one or two. But the student does in time rise above all considerations connected with the mere *personality* of those around him, and so is free from all the injustice and partiality which ordinary love so often brings in its train.

Nor should it for a moment be supposed that in gaining this wide affection for all he loses the especial love for his closer friends. The unusually perfect link between Ananda and the Buddha, as between S. John and Jesus, is on record to prove that on the contrary this is enormously intensified; and the tie between a Master and his pupils is stronger far than any earthly bond. For the affection which flourishes upon the path of holiness is an affection between egos, and not merely between personalities; therefore, it is strong and permanent, without fear of diminution or fluctuation, for it is that "perfect love which casted out fear."

IV. Arahat (the venerable, the perfect). On attaining this level, the aspirant constantly enjoys the consciousness of the buddhic plane and is able to use its powers and faculties while still in the physical body; and when he leaves that body in sleep or trance, he passes at once into the unutterable glory of the nirvanic plane. In this stage the occultist must cast off the last remains of the five remaining fetters, which are:

Ruparaga: desire for beauty of form or for physical existence in a form, even including that in the heaven-world.

Aruparaga: desire for formless life

Mano: pride.

Uddhachcha: agitation or irritability.

10.Avijja: ignorance.

On this we may remark that the casting off of Ruparaga involves not only getting rid of desire for earthly life, however grand or noble that life may be and astral or devachanic life, however glorious, but also of all liability to be unduly influenced or repelled by the external beauty or ugliness of any person or thing.

Aruparaga: desire for life either in the highest and formless planes of the heaven-world or in the still more exalted buddhic plane would be merely a higher and less sensual form of selfishness and must be cast off just as much as the lower. Uddhachcha really means "liability to be disturbed in mind," and a man who had finally cast off this fetter would be absolutely unruffled by anything whatever that might happen to him perfectly impervious to any kind of attack upon his dignified serenity.

The getting rid of ignorance of course implies the acquisition of perfect knowledge, practical omniscience as regards our planetary chain. When all the fetters are finally cast off the advancing ego reaches the fifth stage, the stage of full adept-ship and becomes.

V. Asekha, "the one who has no more to learn," again as regards our planetary chain. It is quite impossible for us to realize at our present level what this attainment means. All the splendor of the nirvanic plane lies open before the waking eyes of the adept, while when he chooses to leave his body, he has the power to enter upon something higher still, a plane which to us is the merest name. As Professor Rhys Davids explains, "He is now free from all sin; he sees and values all things in this life and their true value; all evil being rooted from his mind he experiences only righteous desires for himself and tender pity and regard and exalted love for others."

To show how little he has lost the sentiment of love, we read in the Metta Sutta of the state of mind of one who stands at this level: "As a mother love, who even at the risk of her own life protects her only son, such love let there be toward all beings. Let goodwill without measure prevail in the whole world, above, below, around, unstinted, unmixed with any feeling of differing or opposing interests. When a man remains steadfastly in this state of mind all the while, whether he be standing or walking, sitting, or lying down, then is come to pass the saying which is written, 'Even in this life has holiness been found.' "

- - -

CHAPTER XVII

What Lies Beyond

Beyond this period, it is obvious that we can know nothing of the new qualifications required for the still higher levels which yet lie before the perfect man. It is abundantly clear, however, that when man has become Asekha he has exhausted all the possibilities of moral development, so that further advancement for him can only mean still wider knowledge and still more wonderful spiritual powers. We are told that when man has thus attained his spiritual majority, whether in the slow course of evolution or by the shorter path of self-development he assumes the fullest control of his own destinies and makes choice of his future line of evolution among seven possible paths which he sees opening before him.

Naturally at our present level we cannot expect to understand much about these, and the faint outline of some of them which is all that can be sketched in for us conveys very little to the mind, except that most of them take the adept altogether away from our earth-chain, which no longer affords sufficient scope for his evolution.

One path is that of those who, as the technical phrase goes, "accept Nirvana." Through what incalculable aeons they remain in that sublime condition, for what work they are preparing themselves, what will be their future line of evolution, are questions upon which we know nothing and indeed if information upon such points could be given it is more than likely that it would prove quite incomprehensible to us at our present stage.

But this much at least we may grasp that the blessed state of Nirvana is not, as some have ignorantly supposed, a condition of blank nothingness, but on the contrary of far more intense and beneficent activity; and that ever as man rises higher in the scale of nature his possibilities become greater, his work for others ever grander and more far-reaching, and that infinite wisdom and infinite power mean for him only infinite capacity for service, because they are directed by infinite love.

Another class chooses a spiritual evolution not quite so far removed from humanity, for though not directly connected with the next chain of our system it extends through two long periods corresponding to its first and second rounds, at the end of which time they also appear to "accept Nirvana," but at a higher stage than those previously mentioned.

Others join the deva evolution, whose progress lies along a grand chain consisting of seven chains like ours, each of which to them is as one world. This line of evolution is spoken of as the most gradual and therefore the least arduous of the seven courses; but though it is sometimes referred to in the books as "yielding to the temptation to become a god." it is only in comparison with the sublime height of renunciation of the Nirmanakaya that it can be spoken of in this half-disparaging manner, for the adept who chooses this course has indeed a glorious career before him, and though the path which he selects is not the shortest, it is nevertheless a very noble one.

Yet another group are the Nirmanakayas those who, declining all these easier methods, choose the shortest but steepest path to the heights which still lie before them. They form what is poetically termed the "guardian wall," and, as *The Voice of the Silence* tells us, "protect the world from further and far greater misery and sorrow," not indeed by warding off from its external evil influences, but by devoting all their strength to the work of pouring down upon it a flood of spiritual force and assistance without which it would assuredly be in far more hopeless case than now.

Yet again there are those who remain even more directly in association with humanity, and continue to incarnate among it, choosing the path which leads through the four stages of what we have called above the official period; and among these are the Masters of Wisdom those from whom we who study Theosophy have learnt such fragments as we know of the mighty harmony of evolving Nature. But it would seem that only a certain comparatively small number adopt this course probably only so many as are necessary for the carrying on of this physical side of the work.

In hearing of these different possibilities, people sometimes exclaim rashly that there could of course be no thought in a master's mind of choosing any but that course which most helps humanity, a remark which greater knowledge would have prevented them from making. We should never forget that there are other evolutions in the solar system besides our own, and no doubt it is necessary for the carrying out of the vast plan of the Logos that there should be adepts working on all the seven lines to which we have referred. Surely the choice of the Master would be to go wherever his work was most needed to place his services with absolute selflessness at the disposal of the Powers in charge of this part of the great scheme of evolution.

This then is the path which lies before us, the path which each one of us should be beginning to tread. Stupendous though its heights appear we should remember that they are attained but gradually and step by step and that those who now stand near the summit once toiled in the mire of the valleys, even as we are doing. Although this path may at first seem hard and toilsome, yet ever as we rise our footing becomes firmer and our outlook wider, and thus we find ourselves better able to help those who are climbing beside us.

Because it is at first thus hard and toilsome to the lower self, it has sometimes been called by the very misleading title of "the path of woe;" but, as Mrs. Besant has beautifully written, "through all such suffering there is a deep and abiding joy, for the suffering is of the lower nature, and the joy of the higher." When the last shred of the personality is gone all that can thus suffer has passed away, and in the perfected Adept there is unruffled peace and everlasting joy. He sees the end toward which all is working, and rejoices in that end, knowing that earth's sorrow is but a passing phase in human evolution.

"That of which little has been said is the profound content which comes from being on the path, from realizing the goal and the way to it, from knowing that the power to be useful is increasing, and that the lower nature is being gradually extirpated. And little has been said of the rays of joy which fall upon the path from loftier levels, the dazzling glimpses of the glory to be revealed, the serenity which the storms of earth cannot ruffle. To anyone who has entered on the path all other ways have lost their charm, and its sorrows have a keeper bliss than the best joys of the lower world." (Vahan, vol. v., No. 12.)

Let no man therefore despair because he thinks the task too great for him; what man has done man can do, and just in proportion as we extend our aid to those whom we can help, so will those who have already attained be able in their turn to help us. So, from the lowest to the highest we who are treading the steps of the path are bound together by one long chain of mutual service, and none need feel neglected or alone, for though sometimes the lower flights of the great staircase may be wreathed in mist, we know that it leads up to happier regions and purer air, where the light is always shining.

- - -

LIST OF TITLES WITH ISBN NO.

ISBN	TITLE
9788194914129	1984
9789390575220	1984 & Animal Farm (2In1)
9789390575572	1984 & Animal Farm (2In1): The International Best-Selling Classics
9789390575848	35 Sonnets
9789390575329	A Clergyman's Daughter
9789390575923	A Study In Scarlet
9789390896097	A Tale Of Two Cities
9789390896837	Abide in Christ
9789390896202	Abraham Lincoln
9789390896912	Absolute Surrender
9789390896608	African American Classic Collection
9789390575305	Aldous Huxley: The Collected Works
9789390896141	An Autobiography of M. K. Gandhi
9789390575886	Animal Farm
9789390575619	Animal Farm & The Great Gatsby (2In1)
9789390575626	Animal Farm & We
9789390896158	Anna Karenina
9789390575534	Antic Hay
9789390896165	Antony & Cleopatra
9789390896172	As I Lay Dying
9789390896226	As You like it
9789390575671	At Your Command
9789390575350	Awakened Imagination
9789390575114	Be What You Wish
9789390896233	Believe In yourself
9789390896998	Best of Charles Darwin: The Origin of Species & Autobiography
9789390896684	Best Of Horror : Dracula And Frankenstein
9789390575503	Best Of Mark Twain (The Adventures of Tom Sawyer AND The Adventures of Huckleberry Finn)
9789390896769	Black History Collection
9789390575756	Brave New World, Animal Farm & 1984 (3in1)

9789390896240	Brother Karamzov
9789390575053	Bulleh Shah Poetry
9789390575725	Burmese Days
9789390896257	Bushido
9789390896066	Can't Hurt Me
9788194914112	Chanakya Neeti: With The Complete Sutras
9789390896042	Crime and Punishment
9789390575527	Crome Yellow
9789390575046	Down and Out in Paris and London
9789390896844	Dracula
9789390575442	Emersons Essays: The Complete First & Second Series (Self-Reliance & Other Essays)
9789390575749	Emma
9789390575817	Essential Tozer Collection - The Pursuit of God & The Purpose of Man
9789390896578	Fascism What It Is and How to Fight It
9789390575688	Feeling is the Secret
9789390575190	Five Lessons
9789390575954	Frankenstein
9789390575237	Franz Kafka: Collected Works
9789390575282	Franz Kafka: Short Stories
9789390575060	George Orwell Collected Works
9789390575077	George Orwell Essays
9789390575213	George Orwell Poems
9788194914150	Greatest Poetry Ever Written Vol 1
9788194914143	Greatest Poetry Ever Written Vol 1
9789390896301	Gulliver's Travel
9789390575961	Gunaho Ka Devta
9789390575893	H. P. Lovecraft Selected Stories Vol 1
9789390575978	H. P. Lovecraft Selected Stories Vol 2
9789390896059	Hamlet
9789390575022	His Last Bow: Some Reminiscences of Sherlock Holmes
9789390896134	History of Western Philosophy
9789390575121	Homage To Catalonia

9789390896219	How to develop self-confidence and Improve public Speaking
9789390896295	How to enjoy your life and your Job
9789390575633	How to own your own mind
9789390896318	How to read Human Nature
9789390896325	How to sell your way through the life
9789390896370	How to use the laws of mind
9789390896387	How to use the power of prayer
9789390896028	How to win friends & Influence People
9788194824176	How To Win Friends and Influence People
9789390896103	Humility The Beauty of Holiness
9789390896653	Imperialism the Highest Stage of Capitalism
9789390575084	In Our Time
9789390575169	In Our Time & Three Stories and Ten poems
9789390575145	James Allen: The Collected Works
9789390896189	Jesus Himself
9789390575480	Jo's Boys
9789390896394	Julius Caesar
9789390575404	Keep the Aspidistra Flying
9789390896400	Kidnapped
9789390896424	King Lear
9789390575824	Lady Susan
9789390896455	Law of Success
9789390896264	Lincoln The Unknown
9789390575565	Little Men
9789390575640	Little Women
9788194914174	Lost Horizon
9789390896462	Macbeth
9789390896929	Man Eaters of Kumaon
9789390896523	Man The Dwelling Place of God
9789390896349	Man The Dwelling Place of God
9789390575909	Mansfield Park
9788194914136	Manto Ki 25 Sarvshreshth Kahaniya
9789390896509	Marxism, Anarchism, Communism
9789390575664	Mathematical Principles of Natural Philosophy

9788194914198	Meditations
9789390575800	Mein Kampf
9789390575794	Memory How To Develop, Train, And Use It
9789390896486	Mind Power
9789390896585	Money
9789390575039	Mortal Coils
9789390575770	My Life and Work
9789390896035	Narrative of the Life of Frederick Douglass
9789390575152	Neville Goddard: The Collected Works
9789390575985	Northanger Abbey
9789390896530	Notes From Underground
9789390896547	Oliver Twist
9789390575459	On War
9789390575541	One, None and a Hundred Thousand
9789390896554	Othelo
9789390575435	Out Of This World
9789390575015	Persuasion
9789390575510	Prayer The Art Of Believing
9789390575091	Pride and Prejudice
9789390896561	Psychic Perception
9789390575381	Rabindranath Tagore - 5 Best Short Stories Vol 2
9789390575367	Rabindranath Tagore - Short Stories (Masters Collections Including The Childs Return)
9789390575374	Rabindranath Tagore 5 Best Short Stories Vol 1 (Including The Childs Return
9789390896622	Romeo & Juliet
9789390896127	Sanatana Dharma
9789390575596	Seedtime & Harvest
9789390896639	Selected Stories of Guy De Maupassant
9789390575206	Self-Reliance & Other Essays
9789390575176	Sense and Sensibility
9789390575299	Shyamchi Aai
9789390896738	Socialism Utopian and Scientific
9789390896646	Success Through a Positive Mental Attitude
9789390575428	The Adventures of Huckleberry Finn

9789390575183	The Adventures of Sherlock Holmes
9789390575343	The Adventures of Tom Sawyer
9789390896691	The Alchemy Of Happiness
9789390575862	The Art Of Public Speaking
9789390896288	The Autobiography Of Charles Darwin
9788194914181	The Best of Franz Kafka: The Metamorphosis & The Trial
9789390575008	The Call Of Cthulhu and Other Weird Tales
9789390575107	The Case-Book of Sherlock Holmes
9789390896110	The Castle Of Otranto
9789390896745	The Communist Manifesto
9789390575589	The Complete Fiction of H. P. Lovecraft
9789390575497	The Complete Works of Florence Scovel Shinn
9789390896820	The Conquest of Breard
9789390896813	The Diary of a Young Girl
9789390896332	The Diary of a Young Girl The Definitive Edition of the Worlds Most Famous Diary
9789390575701	The Great Gatsby, Animal Farm & 1984 (3In1)
9789390575312	The Greatest Works Of George Orwell (5 Books) Including 1984 & Non-Fiction
9789390575992	The Hound of Baskervilles
9789390896707	The Idiot
9789390896714	The Invisible Man
9789390575657	The Knowledge of the holy
9789390575558	The Law & the Promise
9789390896721	The Law Of Attraction
9789390896776	The Leader in you
9789390896363	The Life of Christ
9789390896196	The Man-Eating Leopard of Rudraprayag
9789390896783	The Master Key to Riches
9789390575268	The Memoirs Of Sherlock Holmes
9789390896479	The Midsummer Night's Dream
9789390575466	The Mill On The Floss
9789390896790	The Miracles of your mind
9789390896660	The Mutual Aid A Factor in Evolution
9789390896448	The Origin of Species

ISBN	Title
9789390896905	The Peter Kropotkin Anthology The Conquest of Bread & Mutual Aid A Factor of Evolution
9789390896806	The Picture of Dorian Gray
9789390896271	The Picture of Dorian Gray
9789390575275	The Power Of Awareness
9789390896356	The Power of Concentration
9788194824169	The Power of Positive Thinking
9789390575411	The Power of the Spoken Word
9788194914105	The Power Of Your Subconscious Mind
9789390896899	The Power of Your Subconscious Mind
9789390896417	The Principles of Communism
9789390575787	The Psychology Of Mans Possible Evolution
9789390896615	The Psychology of Salesmanship
9789390575732	The Pursuit of God
9789390575398	The Pursuit of Happiness
9789390896851	The Quick and Easy Way to effective Speaking
9789390575947	The Return Of Sherlock Holmes
9789390575138	The Road To Wigan Pier
9789390896981	The Root of the Righteous
9789390575855	The Science Of Being Well
9788194914167	The Science Of Getting Rich, The Science Of Being Great & The Science Of Being Well (3In1)
9789390896011	The Screwtape Letters
9789390896073	The Screwtape Letters
9789390575336	The Secret Door to Success
9789390575695	The Secret Of Imagining
9789390896868	The Secret Of Success
9789390896431	The Seven Last Words
9789390575930	The Sign of the Four
9789390896004	The Sonnets
9789390896516	The Souls of Black Folk
9789390896875	The Sound and The Fury
9789390575244	The State and Revolution
9789390896882	The Story of My Life
9789390896936	The Story Of Oriental Philosophy

9789390896752	The Strange Case of Dr. Jekyll and Mr. Hyde
9789390896943	The Tempest
9789390575916	The Valley Of Fear
9789390575879	The Wind in the willows
9789390896080	The Wind in the willows
9789390575763	Their eyes were watching gofd
9789390575831	Three Stories
9789390896950	Twelfth Night
9789390896592	Twelve Years a Slave
9789390896677	Up from Slavery
9789390896974	Value Price and Profit
9789390896967	Wake Up and Live
9789390896493	With Christ in the School of Prayer
9789390575602	Your Faith is Your Fortune
9789390575473	Your Infinite Power To Be Rich
9789390575251	Your Word is Your Wand
9789390575718	Youth
9789391316099	A Christmas Carol
9789391316105	A Doll's House
9789391316501	A Passage to India
9789391316709	A Portrait of the Artist as a Young Man
9789391316112	A Tale of Two Cities
9789391316747	A Tear and a Smile
9789391316167	Agnes Gray
9789391316174	Alice's Adventures in Wonderland
9789391316136	Anandamath
9789391316181	Anne Of Green Gables
9789391316754	Anthem
9789391316198	Around The World in 80 Days
9789391316013	As A Man Thinketh
9789391316242	Autobiography of a Yogi
9789391316266	Beyond Good and Evil
9789391316761	Bleak House
9789391316778	Chitra, a Play in One Act
9789391316310	David Copperfield

9789391316075	Demian
9789391316785	Dubliners
9789391316051	Favourite Tales from the Arabian Nights
9789391316235	Gitanjali
9789391316068	Gravity
9789391316150	Great Speeches of Abraham Lincoln
9789391316662	Guerilla Warfare
9789391316839	Kim
9789391316822	Mother
9789391316211	My Childhood
9789391316846	Nationalism
9789391316327	Oliver Twist
9789391316853	Pygmalion
9789391316334	Relativity: The Special and the General Theory
9789391316389	Scientific Healing Affirmation
9789391316341	Sons and Lovers
9789391316587	Tales from India
9789391316372	Tess of The D'Urbervilles
9789391316396	The Awakening and Selected Stories
9789391316402	The Bhagvad Gita
9789391316303	The Book of Enoch
9789391316228	The Canterville Ghost
9789391316907	The Dynamic Laws of Prosperity
9789391316006	The Great Gatsby
9789391316860	The Hungry Stones and Other Stories
9789391316433	The Idiot
9789391316440	The Importance of Being Earnest
9789391316297	The Light of Asia
9789391316914	The Madman His Parables and Poems
9789391316457	The Odyssey
9789391316921	The Picture of Dorian Gray
9789391316464	The Prince
9789391316938	The Prophet
9789391316945	The Republic
9789391316518	The Scarlet Letter

9789391316143	The Seven Laws of Teaching
9789391316525	The Story of My Experiments with Truth
9789391316532	The Tales of the Mother Goose
9789391316549	The Thirty Nine Steps
9789391316594	The Time Machine
9789391316600	The Turn of the Screw
9789391316983	The Upanishads
9789391316617	The Yellow Wallpaper
9789391316426	The Yoga Sutras of Patanjali
9789391316990	Ulysses
9789391316624	Utopia
9789391316679	Vanity Fair
9789391316020	What Is To Be Done
9789391316686	Within A Budding Grove
9789391316693	Women in Love